AFRICAN ETHNOGRAPHIC STUDIES
OF THE 20TH CENTURY

I0028008

Volume 57

ARTS OF WEST AFRICA

ARTS OF WEST AFRICA
(Excluding Music)

Edited by
MICHAEL E. SADLER

R Routledge
Taylor & Francis Group

LONDON AND NEW YORK

First published in 1935 by Oxford University Press for the International African Institute.

This edition first published in 2018
by Routledge
2 Park Square, Milton Park, Abingdon, Oxon OX14 4RN

and by Routledge
52 Vanderbilt Avenue, New York, NY 10017

Routledge is an imprint of the Taylor & Francis Group, an informa business

© 1935 International African Institute

British Library Cataloguing in Publication Data
A catalogue record for this book is available from the British Library

ISBN: 978-0-8153-8713-8 (Set)
ISBN: 978-0-429-48813-9 (Set) (ebk)
ISBN: 978-1-138-59763-1 (Volume 57) (hbk)
ISBN: 978-1-138-59772-3 (Volume 57) (pbk)
ISBN: 978-0-429-48681-4 (Volume 57) (ebk)

Publisher's Note
The publisher has gone to great lengths to ensure the quality of this reprint but points out that some imperfections in the original copies may be apparent.

Disclaimer
The publisher has made every effort to trace copyright holders and would welcome correspondence from those they have been unable to trace.

ARTS OF
WEST AFRICA

(EXCLUDING MUSIC)

EDITED BY

MICHAEL E. SADLER

WITH AN INTRODUCTION

BY

SIR WILLIAM ROTHENSTEIN

Published for the
INTERNATIONAL INSTITUTE OF
AFRICAN LANGUAGES AND CULTURES
BY THE OXFORD UNIVERSITY PRESS
LONDON: HUMPHREY MILFORD

OXFORD UNIVERSITY PRESS
AMEN HOUSE, E.C. 4
LONDON EDINBURGH GLASGOW NEW YORK
TORONTO MELBOURNE CAPETOWN BOMBAY
CALCUTTA MADRAS SHANGHAI
HUMPHREY MILFORD
PUBLISHER TO THE UNIVERSITY

FIRST IMPRESSION JANUARY 1935
SECOND IMPRESSION OCTOBER 1935

PRINTED IN GREAT BRITAIN

ACKNOWLEDGEMENTS

IN the course of discussions which took place at the Colonial Office during meetings of the Advisory Committee on Education, the suggestion was made that a short illustrated book on the Arts of West Africa might be of service to many of those who, in this country and overseas, are interested in the life and welfare of that region.

The idea was welcomed by the International Institute of African Languages and Cultures, which assigned from its Publication Fund £100 towards the cost of the preparation and issue of this book.

Examples of African art were chosen by Mr. Edgar Ainsworth (formerly in the Government Service, Malaya), Mr. Richard Carline, and Mr. G. A. Stevens (formerly on the staff of the Prince of Wales's College, Achimota, Gold Coast, and now of Eastbourne College). For this purpose, visits were paid to the following museums and collections: the British Museum; the Wellcome Historical Medical Museum; the Imperial Institute; the Horniman Museum; the Royal United Services Institution; the Cuming Museum (Southwark); the Baptist Missionary Society (Holborn); the Pitt-Rivers Collection (Oxford); the Cambridge University Museum of Ethnology; the Liverpool Free Public Museum; the Bristol Museum; the Royal Albert Memorial Museum (Exeter); the Wisbech Museum; the Newbury Museum; the Bankfield Museum (Halifax); the Brighton Public Museum; and the collections of Captain A. W. F. Fuller and of Mr. Curtis Moffat. To these museums and collectors cordial thanks are given for permission to photograph, and for valuable help in the preparation of descriptive notes.

At the instance of the Colonial Office and of its Advisory Committee on Education, the Empire Marketing Board kindly gave the service of their expert photographers for the production of the plates. This work was done under the expert supervision of Mr. J. Grierson (Empire Marketing Board) with the collaboration of Mr. Edgar Ainsworth, Mr. Richard Carline, and the assistance of Mr. Fletcher of the Empire Marketing

Board, and their photographers, Mr. Davidson and Mr. Cowland (then of the *Studio Sun*).

The British Museum afforded special facilities for the photography of objects, drawn from cases in the Museum, or generously lent for the purpose by other museums and collectors. To the Keeper of the Ethnological Department, British Museum, and to the Directors and Curators of the museums named above, grateful thanks are given.

The valuable descriptions of the objects illustrated in the book are the work of Mr. Richard Carline.

In the initiation of the book indispensable help was given by members of the Advisory Committee on Education and throughout the work of its preparation by Mr. Hanns Vischer, C.B.E., and Mr. Arthur Mayhew, C.I.E., the Secretaries of that Committee.

Special thanks are due to those who have contributed essays to this volume: to Mr. G. A. Stevens and Mr. Gabriel Pippet, both of whom have had experience in the Department of Art, Prince of Wales's College, Achimota, Gold Coast; to Mr. Richard Carline, whose skill and scholarship have produced the catalogue giving an exact description of the objects illustrated by the plates; and to Sir William Rothenstein, Principal of the Royal College of Art, for his Introduction to the volume.

CONTENTS

ACKNOWLEDGEMENTS   v

INTRODUCTION, *by* SIR WILLIAM ROTHENSTEIN, *Principal of the Royal College of Art, South Kensington*   ix

SIGNIFICANCE AND VITALITY OF AFRICAN ART, *by* SIR MICHAEL SADLER, *formerly Master of University College, Oxford*   1

EDUCATIONAL SIGNIFICANCE OF INDIGENOUS AFRICAN ART, *by* G. A. STEVENS, B.A., *The Queen's College, Oxford. Art Master, Eastbourne College and formerly Head of the Department of Art, Prince of Wales's College, Achimota, Gold Goast*   13

TEACHING WOOD-CARVING AT ACHIMOTA, *by* GABRIEL PIPPET   20

ARTS OF WEST AFRICA, 32 Plates, *with descriptive notes by* RICHARD CARLINE   23

BIBLIOGRAPHY OF INDIGENOUS ART IN WEST AFRICA, *by* SIR MICHAEL SADLER   97

INTRODUCTION

By SIR WILLIAM ROTHENSTEIN
Principal of the Royal College of Art

THE purpose of this book is to draw attention to something underlying the material lives of races with whom Europeans have come into close relations. This present venture is the result of the anxiety felt lest a precious inheritance be lost through lack of knowledge among those who take up the burden of government.

We have learned how destructive the impact of a highly organized civilization can be on the ritual, social customs and the arts of a less advanced one. Indeed there are pages of history so painful to follow that our faculty for forgetting alone saves us from despair. We now know, better than our fathers and grandfathers, the value that attaches to the art of every people. But even those most aware of its importance are uncertain how the arts are best encouraged and preserved.

Africa and slavery were, little more than a century ago in Europe, and half a century in the United States, closely connected. That the white man had anything to learn from the black man was unsuspected. A century ago, *art* meant Greek and Italian art. The arts of India, China, and Japan were 'curiosities', the interest in African and other 'savage' carvings was purely ethnological.

During the last fifty years a new understanding of Eastern art has been growing, but to the present generation is due the discovery of the aesthetic aspect of African and primitive American culture. The soldier, engineer, civil servant and trader are now followed by the antique dealer, with his offer of new lamps for old; and new lamps in the shape of the products of Europe are greedily accepted in exchange. But just as the foreign grey squirrel, once it is introduced, gradually ousts the native red squirrel, so do our imports disturb the native crafts. Thereafter our consciences are apt to prick us, and educationalists are consulted. How can the little that still survives of the old vision and cunning of hand be preserved in Africa, and how should they be continued?

INTRODUCTION

It is a difficult problem to face. We have witnessed the evil influence of bad European models on indigenous arts; while the exploitation of so-called native crafts has led only to another kind of cheap commercialism. The real difficulty lies in the crumbling of the religious and tribal systems under which the native arts grew up. To encourage the mere copying of native craftsmanship when the influences which shaped and vitalized it are dead seems fruitless. Something more active is needed.

Now negro art was even more closely connected with religious observance than the art of Europe. Its basis was not primarily aesthetic. Indeed we know little or nothing of the primitive aesthetic impulse; our experience of children's drawings, which now delight us with their directness of form, colour and observation, tells us that while children have no conscious aesthetic sense, their instinctive taste and imagination give an immediate reality to their naïve compositions which professional artists rarely attain. We know, too, that the child who delights us with his drawings at ten will probably set our teeth on edge at twenty years of age.

Here lies our problem. Understanding of the negro genius for form has come to us but lately: it reached us from Paris; yet for years we had the opportunity, at the Ethnological Section of the British Museum, of discovering it for ourselves. We looked on the carved gods, the masks, and weapons as curiosities merely, not as works of art.

We have enlightened men and women with knowledge enough to understand and encourage signs of promise, however unlike the usual educationalist's views of correctness they may be. A few of these should ensure that any instruction given would be in sympathy with the racial spirit. To impose any other form of teaching would be fatal to it.

The results of Mr. Stevens's short stay at Achimota show a vitality, a happy enjoyment of nature, which survive in the young African. Here is a hopeful basis to work on. To my mind this quick spirit need not show itself in the forms which, from our knowledge of connoisseurs' collections, we associate with African art. As Sir Michael Sadler points out in his article, the ritualistic beliefs which dictated the forms of the

x

older carvings are giving place to new conceptions of life and death. Form and style are likely to follow, as they have always done in the past, on the artist's impulse to copy the life about him. Mr. Stevens's pioneer work must be continued, if the latent artistic faculties are again to grow and flourish in Africa. The African has preserved his strong sense of pattern; do not let us weaken it by putting before the young the dreary outlines of chairs, jugs and candlesticks, which are still to be found as examples to be copied in Indian elementary schools.

I hesitate to touch on the political aspect of the matter; but to take in hand the guidance of a politically backward people is to assume a grave responsibility. Marshal Lyautey has shown in Morocco that administrative charge includes, first and foremost, respect for, and energetic protection of, native culture. We may do worse than study the methods of the great Frenchman.

SIGNIFICANCE AND VITALITY OF AFRICAN ART

By SIR MICHAEL SADLER

THE examples of carving and other handiwork which are illustrated in this volume have, with one exception, been drawn from West Africa. They are from the regions between Senegal and Angola. But the majority of the works which have been chosen for reproduction come from British territories—Gambia, Sierra Leone, the Gold Coast, Nigeria, and the British sphere of the Cameroons. West Africa, as a whole, has regional unity in plastic art. Its sculpture, handicraft, and design are differentiated from the corresponding arts in the other divisions of the continent south of the Sahara. In the sphere of art West Africa is coherent. But within its compass there are outstanding tribal or territorial characteristics. Convincing evidence of this differentiation is given by the monumental heads of Gabun, by the bronzes of Benin, by the sensitive sculpture of the Ivory Coast and the French Sudan, and by the masks and carved figures of the Portuguese Congo. These regions especially, but by no means exclusively, have produced masterpieces which have won the admiration of artists and critics in Europe and America.

At many points in West Africa there are, it is true, signs of the infiltration of artistic ideas from other regions. Examples of this infiltration are found in the designs of the State chairs used by the chiefs in Ashanti, the construction of which shows European lineage. Another example may possibly be found in the panelled doors of Benin which, in the ground plan of their arrangement, show signs of a European prototype. There are also traces of Nilotic influence in some of the carvings made in French Sudan. But these streaks of external influence are of relatively small importance in the artistic work of West Africa. Allowing for regional differences in feeling and tradition, we may say that the carving, the wooden sculpture, and the textile design of this great division of the continent form an impressive artistic whole. Nor are its salient characteristics weakened by the fact that the indigenous art of West Africa presents at certain points analogies to primitive art in other regions of the world. For example, in some of the masks from the Belgian Congo the design is analogous to forms found in Malaya. Some of the bead-work from the Cameroons recalls the mats made in Sumatra. An ancient tombstone found in Guinea has a parallel in Hawaii. A lion covered with metal plates by a craftsman in Dahomey resembles an example of early Chinese sculpture. But these likenesses are not derivative. They are due to the affinities disclosed in all primitive art. West Africa has made its own characteristic contribution to the artistic treasures of the world.

Of singular beauty among the works illustrated in this volume are the wooden mask from the Ivory Coast, now in the Bristol Museum, which has a poignancy like that of French Gothic sculpture of the twelfth century; the unornamented calabash believed to have come from Fernando Po and now in the Cuming Museum at Southwark; the group of figures crowning with monumental dignity the base of the pedestal of the harp from Nigeria; the spears from the Congo; the paddles and agricultural implements from Angola; the stools from Ashanti; the head-rests from Dahomey; the kneeling figure of a woman holding a seat upon her upstretched hands, which comes from the Congo; the little gold weight from Ashanti, representing two figures carrying a chief in a litter. These are all consummate in design. Impressive through the balanced disposition of its rich ornament is the painted earthenware vessel, with figures modelled in relief on its base and lid, which is believed to have come from Dahomey and is now in the Bankfield Museum in Halifax. Simpler and even more effective in design is the relief of snakes and frogs on the base of the black earthenware vessel from Ashanti, now in the British Museum. In the textile patterns, alike from Ashanti and the Congo, the designs have either a freedom which is not undisciplined or a simplicity which does not become monotonous. Races alone with a rich faculty for design and sculpture could have made things so beautiful as these.

Less readily welcomed by eyes accustomed to European art is the wooden figure from Nigeria, of a mother carrying children on her hip and shoulders. Here the design is simplified with mastery of thrust and resistance but with disregard of accuracy in anatomical detail. The great feet serve not only to prolong the base of the stool but give power and elasticity to the bending figure which, with resilient force, bears the weight of the clinging children. The sculptor has seized the essentials of the group. In strong expressive shape he conveys to us the muscular strain to which the mother willingly submits. The curves respond to one another; the angles of the arms and legs accord with the rhythm of the pattern: and the strong vertical line which runs from the top of her head down the back of the seated figure is carried through the post of the stool firmly to the ground.

A second example, in this case of Yoruba sculpture (Western Nigeria), shows the vital power of the West African sculptor, although in a form which is not obedient to the canons of European art. This hieratic figure probably represents the mother-goddess of earth, Odudua, one of whose chief temples was at Ado, north-west of Lagos. Seated upon a stool the goddess holds in her right hand a disk-headed fan; with her left she supports the back of a child whose legs are stretched out across her knees. The handle of her fan rests upon the head of a seated attendant, whose diminutive form gives unearthly height and solemn majesty to the great figure of the seated goddess and her child. Hanging above the breast of the goddess and suspended from her shoulders by a broad necklace of cords is a symbolic rod. The hair is dressed close to the head, helmet-wise, with a high dividing crest. The enigmatic expression on the face of the goddess gives to the onlooker a feeling of her mysterious withdrawal; hers transcends human experience. But the child on her lap is alert, and like the dog below him, watchful of bystanders. Links between the worshipper and the goddess are found in the little watchful attendant, the prick-eared dog, and the quietly observant child. The lines of these three mediate forms lead the eye upward to the hushed mysterious countenance of the goddess herself. The sculptor has disregarded accuracy of proportion and of anatomical form. The child is full of life and character, but the legs are left unseparated in the block of wood, though this may perhaps represent the immobility of swaddling clothes. The

3

head is out of proportion to the body; toes and fingers are indicated by deep-cut parallel lines. From the animated vitality of the seated figures on its base and of the child on its mother's knee rises the form of the goddess, mysteriously aloof, impenetrably tranquil, and yet a living presence.

Thus, in order to appreciate the strange beauty of the masterpieces of West African sculpture, we need to put ourselves as near as may be to the place of those for whom the artist carved his figure. What is greatest in West African art is religious. The monumental things, small in scale but great in conception, have been made for worship and awe. It is impossible for us Europeans to evoke from our own thoughts the fears and hopes of African religion. Much which was implied by what the sculptor did or left undone, the significance of his symbolism, the ancestral associations of his forms, must lie beyond the reach of our interpretation. We are remote from much that is evil in it but also from much that is good. These works, vibrating with power, spoke to those for whom they were made with a meaning which we can never fully understand. They belong to an age which is passing, which has nearly passed. Except for those who are already old, they have lost much of their pristine authority. But by another road than that of religious belief we can reach an understanding of their significance. The students of primitive religion, the recorders of primitive beliefs, have given us at any rate the key to the meaning of much that is symbolical and hieratic in West African sculpture. Read with the sculpture before us, the details of primitive religion are revitalized. Thoughts and feelings which the artist has infused into his work become intelligible to us and in their turn transfigure the sculpture, which at first seemed repellent or grotesque. Much of it indeed, like many of the masks from the Congo, becomes, as we concentrate our thoughts upon its form and meaning, even more horrible and terrible than when we first gave it a cursory glance. There are depths of cruelty in primitive religion. Spectres and bloodshed haunt much of West African sculpture. But there are elements in the indigenous faiths of West Africa into the understanding of which we can enter because they embody universal human experience. We too,

4

like the Africans, have a sense of the mystery of things. Like them we feel that there is a bond between our spirit and the spirits of other living things. We are conscious of something present but hidden, powerful but not unfriendly, which is fundamental in our experience, participant in the spirit of something universal yet related to us; something which we divine without definition; the dim background of all knowledge and insight and creative will. In us, though stiff with disuse and overlaid by other habits of thought and feeling, there is something akin to the primitive which makes it possible for us to enter into the thoughts, hopes, and apprehensions of primitive man:

> from outward forms to win
> the passion and the life, whose fountains are within.

More sinister is the skin-covered head with three faces which probably came from the Cameroons and is now in the Horniman Museum. This figure was probably used as a standard or head-piece in the ritual of a secret society which propitiated ancestors at seed-time and harvest with the purpose of enhancing the fruitfulness of the crops and the fertility of the tribe. This work is malign but masterly, as are the skin-covered heads probably from Southern Nigeria and now in the Wellcome Historical Medical Museum, and the initiation mask from the Congo with its ghastly portrayal of death. Repulsive and terrifying but superbly conceived is the white mask (from Southern Nigeria) with eyes ringed with scarlet seeds. This mask was used in religious dances for the propitiation of ghosts in the worship of ancestors. The artists who made them were masters of the macabre.

In the sculpture of West Africa, masks for ceremonial use form the category in which all but the very finest works are found. Supreme among the examples of West African plastic art are some of the long-necked heads from Gabun; the red terra-cotta head called 'Mia' found by Leo Frobenius in Ife, Nigeria;[1] the bronze hunter from Benin;[2] the head of the great fetish Baluba from the Belgian Congo;[3] the head

[1] Figured in E. von Sydow's *Die Kunst der Naturvölker und der Vorzeit* (Propyläen-Kunst-Geschichte, plate 93).

[2] Now in the Museum für Völkerkunde,

Berlin, figured in W. Hausenstein, *Barbaren und Klassiker*, Plate 71.

[3] Figured in A. Portier and F. Poncetton, *Les Arts sauvages, Afrique*, Plate xii.

5

of the fetish with a collar of nails, from Manyema in the French Congo;[1] the woman supporting a round table on her head and lifted fingers from Baluba in the Belgian Congo;[2] the stylized head of an antelope from the country of the Bambaras on the Niger;[3] the brass figure of a man with clenched teeth which came from Dahomey;[4] the ancestral figure of a seated woman holding with bent arms and outstretched fingers a cup, the stalk of which rests between her thighs, from Urua in the eastern district of the Congo;[5] the ovoid head with beetling brow reproduced (without note of provenance) in Carl Einstein's *Negerplastik*, plates 14–15; and the kneeling figure of the Baluba beggar-woman holding a bowl to her breast between outstretched hands from the Belgian Congo.[6]

Very little behind these outstanding achievements, and in some cases equalling them in power, come the masks. Here in the power of arousing terror the sculptors of the Congo are supreme. But it is the Ivory Coast that shows the widest range of creative skill and feeling in mask-design. Some of these works (oval-faced girls with fine-edged features) all but speak, so vivid are they in portraiture. Other masks from the same region are grotesque and formidable but not sinister.[7] A third type of mask is fantastic, like the head of a fish from Amisaka in Southern Nigeria and now in the Pitt-Rivers Museum at Oxford. Vivid and masterful rather than repellent are the two wooden masks which came from Lagos and are now in the Brighton Public Museum. These represent strong-lipped determined women and are hollow in order that they may be worn over the dancer's face.

The mask is the central point in the paraphernalia of the ritual dance or processional ceremony. Its characteristics are a clue to the temperament of the tribe or society which used it. Cruelty in initiation and sacrifice, or the milder mood of solemnity and mumming disguise, express themselves clearly in the art of the mask. To wear the mask is for

[1] A. Portier and F. Poncetton, *Les Arts sauvages, Afrique*, Pl. xv.

[2] Ibid., Pl. xvi.   [3] Ibid., Pl. xxiv.

[4] Ibid., Pl. xxxi.

[5] Figured in Eckart von Sydow, *Kunst und Religion der Naturvölker*, Pl. 15.

[6] J. Maes and H. Lavachery, *L'Art nègre*, Pl. 21.

[7] A long series is reproduced in Portier and Poncetton, *Les Arts sauvages, Afrique*, Pls. xxxii–xlvi.

the time to conceal personality. By becoming something else, by participating in the being of the ancestor or of the animal portrayed, the mask wearer is temporarily freed from the conventional restraints of common life. From behind the mask he or she may sing or say what in ordinary circumstances could not acceptably be said. The dance is a liberation of personality, and to wear the mask is to enjoy privilege of disguise.

'The indigenous art of Africa is above all things stamped with the associations of religion.' In this fact lay its power. But the same fact explains its decay and is the presage of its doom. The tribal religions of West Africa cannot permanently survive the disintegrating acids of science or the impact of European and American teaching and example. In its traditional forms the genius of West Africa has expressed itself in many masterpieces, not to speak of the high level of its customary skill. But the axe has been laid at the root of the tree. What was definite in indigenous belief has become blurred, doubtful, and discredited. The atmosphere of awe and fear is changing, has indeed already changed among multitudes of the people. Thus the conditions which fostered the older art are passing away, and will not return. With them is passing the art which was sustained by the ancient tradition of ritual and worship.

'But', it may be said, 'the West African is by nature fundamentally religious. Into the new order of things he will carry over the characteristics of his temperament. With his old fervour he will embrace and follow a religion new to him but purer than the old. And to the call of his new faith his artistic genius will respond, finding once again the support and patronage which for the time have dwindled. In Europe the Christian Faith won art to its service. What happened in Europe will happen in Africa. The churches will give a new impulse to West African art.'

Possibly this hope, or part of this hope, may come true. Nothing better could happen for the arts of Africa. But there is great unlikeness between the divided Christianity of to-day and the all-embracing authority of the medieval Church. And the Christian Churches in West Africa, like the Christian Churches in Europe, are to-day not likely to offer an early and

7

eager welcome to sculpture conceived and executed in the best tradition of West African art. The Christian Churches have their own artistic traditions, or in some cases a not less deeply rooted repugnance to ornament. And it is only within the last thirty years that works by indigenous sculptors and carvers in West Africa have been acclaimed by many European artists and critics of eminent and indisputable authority for the masterpieces which they are. Perception of the vitality of African sculpture is still far from being universal in Europe. Appreciation of its significant and impressive beauty grows apace, and has (so far as can be judged) the future on its side. But it may be long before the merits of West African sculpture are realized by Europeans in West Africa itself. The day of sincere and discriminating appreciation may be distant. But there is little time to lose. The shadows are falling fast on what is best in West African art. It is to be feared that recognition of the high merit of indigenous African sculpture may come too late.

What then can we do? 'Send,' some may urge, 'as soon as funds allow, to each British dependency in Equatorial Africa, and especially in the West, an artist of outstanding capacity who has shown insight into the significant quality of African art, and who can judge between what is good and what is indifferent or bad in it with the masterly penetration shown twelve years ago by Mr. Roger Fry when he wrote for the *Athenaeum* the memorable article on "Negro Sculpture", since republished in his *Vision and Design*.[1] Or such a man as the late Vernon Blake, who contributed in 1927 an illuminating chapter on "The Aesthetic of Ashanti" to Captain Rattray's classic book on *Religion and Art in Ashanti*.[2] Make it the duty of the artist thus chosen to review all the indigenous arts of the province, its carving, its sculpture, its pottery, its weaving, its metal-work, its dancing and, if his technical knowledge allows, that fundamental African art —its music. Let him study the technique of the indigenous craftsmen and artists, as Captain Rattray studied the technique of the weavers, the potters, the wood-carvers, and the metal-workers of Ashanti. Let him

---

[1] Published by Chatto & Windus. In the edition of 1920 the article referred to is at p. 65.

[2] Oxford University Press, Vernon Blake's chapter is at pp. 344–81.

8

talk with all and sundry, Africans and Europeans, and excite a general interest, even to the point of fierce controversy, in the profound problems which are implicated in the study of African art. Let him commend if he can, criticize or censure if he must, the work of the schools in this branch of education. Let him raise the real issues and fight his battle against stereotyped tradition and against what he holds to be artistic misjudgement. Enable him to exhibit, in various places in the province and with full public explanation, examples of what is really fine in West African art; charge him not to confine himself to examples still obtainable in the province but make it possible for him to procure from the great European collections in Paris, England, Belgium, and Berlin good reproductions of some of the outstanding masterpieces of African sculpture, pottery, and metal-work. And encourage him to supplement these exhibits with a wide range of photographs of indigenous art and design. Public opinion has to be stirred and challenged. The African has been told so long and so often that his art is childish, ignorant, ugly, and grotesque, that he cannot be blamed for misjudging his own inheritance and thinking less highly of it than he ought to think. To know that men in Europe, men whose judgement he cannot but respect, regard the masterpieces of indigenous African sculpture as works of outstanding significance and value would predispose many Africans to see in a new light the artistic possibilities of their own country.'

And there are some, perhaps, who would go farther even than this. 'Do', they might urge, 'in each British dependency in West Africa what has already been done in Mexico by the Government of the country, and done with consummate and memorable success. Enlist a small corps of artists and craftsmen and send them out to preach by example and precept, a new art-gospel in the schools. In part of West Africa, as in Mexico, you have a population with an instinctive turn for expression through art. Set the teachers and their pupils to express themselves freely through art. Give them pictures of the great things their fellow-countrymen have made in past days. Make them understand how highly those great things are now prized and praised by good judges in Europe. In things artistic, which are no mean part of education, try them with freedom. Your experiment may fail, but, on the other hand, as has actually happened in Mexico, it may be a triumphant success.'[1]

To taking this bold course, there is, I feel, a serious objection, the weight of which can be judged only by those whose knowledge of the inner life of West Africa is much closer than mine can ever be. It springs from a difficulty which did not exist in Mexico in the same form or in the same degree. The difficulty in the way, so far as West Africa is concerned, is not administrative but, if I may use the words, moral and cultural. The arts of West Africa, the plastic arts, are by immemorial tradition bound up with forms of religious belief which should not receive renewed and emphatic recognition from Government, and with habits of mind which are so inimical to scientific observation and reasoning that (whatever be the kernel of truth which lies at the heart of them) they have forfeited all claim to support from progressive minds in a modern community. So long as the plastic arts are entangled with superstition, and so long as the allurement of those superstitions retains any measure of power, it would be against the public interest to reinforce their obsolescent authority by an artistic propaganda, which, through the schools, might imprint on the minds of children a wrong conception of the validity of the claims of those superstitions upon their capacity for belief, and tempt them to the renewal of ritual habits from which their elders are shaking themselves free.

Mexico, for this reason, does not afford a precedent for action in West Africa. In the latter, a gap may be needed between the old and the new. When the gap is wide enough it will be safe to employ to the utmost the machinery of educational freedom in the interest of indigenous art and for the sake of all the happiness and well-being which the practice and appreciation of art may bring.

And unfortunately the same difficulty applies to giving untrammelled encouragement through the schools to those most universal of the indigenous arts of West Africa, music, dancing, and song. These are

---

[1] For an account of what has been done in Mexico, well and abundantly illustrated in colour and in black and white, see *Mono-* *grafia de las Escuelas de Pintura al Aire Libre* (Publicaciones de la Secretaria de Educacion Publica—Editorial 'Cultura', Mexico, 1926).

indeed among the fundamental things in education everywhere, and not least in West Africa. The last thing I mean to suggest is their exclusion from the schools. Encouragement, systematic encouragement, of indigenous music and dancing is what would bring education in West Africa into line with the most progressive kinds of education in Europe and the United States. And such encouragement may, under wise conditions, safely be given, because happily it is possible to purge what is sung of what is improper, and to be rid of anything which makes dancing undesirable. The essential things in song and in dancing make for health of body and of mind. In them and in music the artistic genius of Africa expresses itself in the most universal manner. No other arts make so general an appeal. None are more fundamental in early education: none have a wider social value among adults.

The art of music, the art of song, and the art of dancing stand out therefore as having primary value for the communal life of Africa. They are the medium through which rejoicing and sorrow best express themselves. They are the natural and appropriate vehicle for encouragement, for dramatic narrative, for consolation, for stimulus, and for humorous and satiric comment on passing events. It is through these arts, more than through its plastic masterpieces, that Africa has already influenced the mind and habits of Europe and the West. The recording of true African music for the gramophone deserves the warmest encouragement. Many records of genuine quality have already been made available, but a wide field of African music still awaits accurate reproduction. Music is one of the universal languages. It is the artistic language through which Africa will most effectively speak to the world and through which Europe will speak to Africa.

'To my many good friends among the chiefs and people of Ashanti,' Captain Rattray wrote in 1927, 'I have only one message. Guard the national soul of your race and never be tempted to despise your past. Therein, I believe, lies the sure hope that your sons and daughters will one day make their own original contributions to knowledge and progress.' These words may well ring in the thoughts of all Europeans who have learnt to love what is great and good in the arts of West Africa, and who try to see in true perspective the service which those arts may render, not only to Africa itself, but to those whose homes are in distant lands. Out of the past, purged so far as may be of what was amiss, springs what is vital for the future. And through religion and art, as well as through science and mathematics, the mind and soul of man apprehend reality.

EDUCATIONAL SIGNIFICANCE OF INDIGENOUS AFRICAN ART

By G. A. STEVENS

THOSE who are engaged in educational practice in West Africa may feel that this book is of little use to them in their everyday work. It is hoped that what follows will convince them that it is of the utmost value, not merely as an introduction, but as a constant guide and inspiration for their efforts. Such is the conviction not of a theorist but of a practising teacher, one who spent three years in West Africa, in the day-to-day work of teaching classes of students in a Government Training College for Teachers. What is here written is the experience of one in the front line of education, confronted day by day with the same problems, limitations, and difficulties as those are who are still in the field.

First of all, I must say with emphasis that art, such as is illustrated here, had a profound formative effect on my own attitude to art and its relation to education. Without that influence my work might have been quite different, might even not have been done at all. I went to Africa with certain deeply rooted convictions which my experience there proved to be justified.

In art of any value there is a direct connexion between inspiration and formal beauty. In more simple language the artist must believe profoundly in what he is doing, and the beauty which he achieves in his material is the direct result of that belief. Primitive art is the most pure, most sincere form of art there can be, partly because it is deeply inspired by religious ideas and spiritual experience, and partly because it is entirely unselfconscious as art; there are no tricks which can be acquired by the unworthy, and no technical exercises which can masquerade as works of inspiration. Therefore I felt that in contemplating works such as are illustrated here, one was face to face with something extremely precious, a form which was a perfect vehicle for the artistic genius of the African people in the primitive state. That the formal beauty was the

13

direct result of tremendous inspiration seemed the only hypothesis which could account for the fact that some of the most beautiful of these creations were constructed of the poorest flimsiest material—soft wood, feathers, straw, rusty nails, and bits of broken mirrors.

Just because of this dependence of form on inspiration, one was forced to realize that these traditional artistic forms could never be so perfect again. Once the self-contained beliefs and values which are peculiar to primitive society are upset, so the forms in which they have clothed themselves disintegrate. The more complete the civilizing process has been, the more completely destroyed the older arts are. Is not this the experience of every European in Africa? The attitude of sophistication and ridicule towards indigenous art is everywhere, even in the remotest bush village. Or else the artist is admired in the wrong way for his dexterity. There are those who are not artists, who look at the forms of art from the outside, as it were, as examples of craftsmanship; they would seek to revive the old forms and processes without concerning themselves with the old spirit. To the artist this could only be a vulgar sham, because to him a work of art has value only as evidence of a spiritual state.

Nevertheless, as a teacher, one was forced to think of the present and the future. And here, again as a result of the contemplation of indigenous art, one reached another important conviction, namely that the artistic genius of a people was one thing, but the form in which it expressed itself was another, and, ultimately, of lesser importance. In spite of all the sentimental despair of intellectuals in Europe, deploring the decay of primitive art under the influence of our civilization, I found it impossible to believe that the African negro whom I had to teach was an entirely different being from his immediate ancestors, may be, grandparents, who had gone undisturbed in their ways and created masterpieces. One had only to compare examples of African primitive art with examples of primitive art from anywhere else to realize at once that it was permeated with originality of character which made African wood-carving, weaving, and pottery somehow different. It was in this difference that one was able to realize intuitively just what those peculiarly 'African' qualities were, and how really independent they were of limitations of material, technical processes and the like. One came to believe, rightly or wrongly, that what the African had done once in one form he could do again in another.

Thus, one could face the practical work of teaching fortified by two correlated convictions, namely:

(1) that there could be no art of any value without real inspiration;
(2) that the peculiar characteristics of the African artistic genius were likely to continue in whatever form of art was found most suitable.

New 'forms' there were in abundance. There was scarcely an African who had been anywhere near a school who had not been acquainted with 'Hand and Eye' or 'Brushwork' as the elementary mechanics of European drawing, painting, modelling, and handicraft were called. As these exercises had now been taught for half a century, there were many Africans who had achieved considerable ability in them. They knew something of light and shade, mixing of colours, accurate observation of proportions, and perspective—though even the most competent never really mastered this last. There was considerable regard for the subject as an asset in examinations; a fairly widespread vulgar pleasure in imitative skill; very little power of selection between one kind of subject and another, and no attempt to represent living or moving forms. Modelling, which was the only one of these activities which at all resembled an indigenous art, they tended to despise as it was 'dirty' and savoured of the 'bush' which they had left behind. There was certainly no intense delight or excitement in all this schoolwork.

Nevertheless there were certain very interesting qualities in all this work which over and over again proved to me that, however much you try (and we have made a good try), you can never quite destroy the artistic genius of a people. They delighted in patterns of shading which bore no relation to the laws of light on objects, but which seemed to me to echo the dramatic sharpness of planes in the old wood-carving. They loved to exploit the qualities of a soft lead-pencil and make their drawings like polished grates, again an echo of their peculiar feeling for textures and surface qualities. They revelled in heavy masses of colour, particularly in the more exciting metallic pigments with which Europe

15

supplied them, and loved to introduce masses of black and white into their colour—an echo of much of the indigenous weaving. Their love of pattern, of which there is abundant evidence in this book, showed itself in the elaboration of an imaginary gilt frame around their drawings, or in the copying of highly ornamental texts in Gothic lettering. In fact they would be artists instead of applying themselves to the solemn business of training their hands and eyes. These 'faults' were, of course, discouraged by European inspectors, but I believe many native teachers secretly abetted their pupils in their desires.

Could one ever introduce into such an atmosphere a new and worthy inspiration that would set free the artistic impulse which one felt sure was there? One attempted to approach these students first of all with photographs such as these. The result was immediate ridicule and genuine surprise that I should take such 'crude' work seriously. Their ancestors had not been to school, had not received 'Hand and Eye', and therefore could not draw! To hint that perspective was not a *sine qua non* of good drawing was almost blasphemy.

In casting about for something worth while in which these students could really believe, my eye lighted on certain sketches with which they decorated their dormitories. These were done 'out of school', and here they had fairly let themselves go. Under the tremendous excitement of representing the unfortunate 'Mensah falling downstairs with a pail' or the pomp and circumstance which accompanied the 'Housemaster embarking for England', the barren exercises in 'Hand and Eye' had been absorbed in their proper place, and something approaching a work of art was the result. These sketches were a sincere attempt by the students to express their reactions to the whole complex of their immediate surroundings; here was something which, as it developed, could attain the dignity of the older art, a new 'form' to them, it is true, but all the more exciting for being new, and filled out with a graphic meaning which no European could give. How long these had been going on one did not know. The tragedy of it all is that European educational officials could not see their value before.

Obviously there was only one thing to be done and that was to bring this kind of drawing right into the class-room, to take it seriously but not solemnly. At first we did the same kind of thing 'in school'. Then, gradually, by suggesting a greater variety of out-of-door and everyday subjects, one was able to wean them from the more personal and scandalizing cartoon, to something which was dignified by the name of imaginative composition. Drawing from observed objects was no longer called 'copying' but was confined either to objects, generally native in character, which were interesting in themselves, or to exercises in the analysis of form and appearance of objects as closely related as possible to what they needed for their compositions. We also included in our list of observable objects for drawing, flowers, plants, trees, buildings, animals, and human beings. But the carrying out of a definite and worthy subject was always made the most important part of a student's work and had the most time allotted to it.

To those who are not artists this may not seem a very big change. But actually it was a complete revolution of aims and values. People who are not artists and yet who have to teach the subject almost invariably make the mistake of fastening on the mechanics of art while neglecting or ignoring the psychological processes which go to make a work of art and the development of the artist.

It was hard work getting the tradition established, and the greatest opposition came from the older students themselves. The younger generation, however, were won over by their realizing how much more exciting it was to be able to draw a greater variety of subjects, and by discovering that, curiously enough, their drawing, when necessary, became more skilful and accurate.

But the most important result for the purposes of this argument was, that as each generation of students refined on the last and acquired more mastery, so the finished work bore less and less resemblance to second-rate European drawing and more and more resemblance to the forms of the older indigenous art. The same love of clear design, rich pattern, rather precious surface quality, tremendous solidity, and appreciation of volumes; the same characteristics in the treatment of the human figure—large head and small bent legs—all came about, in these drawings, as if the race spirit, after lying dormant for so long, had found itself again.

So much so was this apparent that, two years later, when Captain Rattray asked me to illustrate his volume of Ashanti folk-tales, I immediately turned the task over to a group of my students. Thus was effected a linking-up with the past and a linking-up of two arts at the same time. I was amazed to think how rapidly we had got through the superficial veneer that our civilization is, and how, under proper guidance, African art is so well able to take care of itself.

One of the most gratifying experiences I had was that such results gradually won over even these sophisticated and urbane students to a new respect for and appreciation of their own indigenous art. During my teaching, I had not neglected to show them reproductions of the finest work done in the European tradition, and not only in that tradition, but in the Asiatic and Egyptian also, as I was anxious to destroy the illusion that everything good came out of Europe. In a series of talks I had tried to show them how each people in turn had produced their own art and culture, how continuous each one was, even when it absorbed outside influences, and how they regarded their past achievements with pride. Thus we got back by devious routes to our own West Africa. Could any good thing come out of Nazareth?

I remember one day I was showing a class a series of reproductions of European and other work. It was only a few minutes left over at the end of a lesson and I was not lecturing. They showed such polite and intelligent interest as was expected of them, as each picture in turn came up for inspection. Then, without warning, I turned up a photograph of two magnificent Congo masks. Immediately there came from the whole class that exclamation of surprise mingled with awe and admiration which all who have been in West Africa know so well—'E—yeeh . . . !'

On another occasion I was lecturing to a class of teachers on a refresher course. The subject was 'Hand and Eye Training'. On the table in front of me I had an ordinary black cooking-pot which I had asked a dear old lady in Ashanti to make for me. I had watched it being made and seen her build it up on the ground—no measurement, no callipers, no wheel.

I was telling my audience all this, and then, to clinch matters, I placed the pot against the blackboard and drew, with chalk, a circle on the board round the rim of the pot. With a pair of compasses I then drew another circle on the board, roughly the same size as the first. The slightness of the discrepancy between the two circles astonished even myself; but the effect on my hearers was immediate. They just sat back and gasped. One felt that the last shreds of disrespect for 'bush' art were vanishing away.

TEACHING WOOD-CARVING AT ACHIMOTA

By GABRIEL PIPPET

IT was decided to start teaching wood-carving at Achimota. The Principal had found a reliable African wood-carver in a village in the interior, who he thought would be a useful man for giving instruction, and one whose work showed little, if any, trace of European influence. He came up and we started work in September 1931.

Very few of the boys had done any carving at home. It was important, it seemed to me, that we should get to work with African tools and in the African manner of carving. I was a little apprehensive at first, as the handling of tools and mode of procedure are so different from what I had been accustomed to, and moreover look so dangerous to hands and fingers. But I need not have worried.

I started the carving-master with a demonstration before each of the classes. I was impressed by his exhibition. Before going farther, I should say a word as to how Africans go to work with their simple tools, and describe the tools themselves.

The carver squats on a low block of wood with a like block in front of him between his feet; or, if he is carving a large object, he may have it on the ground itself. He holds this with one hand and gets to work with a large knife—a cutlass they call it—and rapidly roughs it out, using this tool like a chopper: a most effective tool in the hands of a capable man, but one requiring great precision. I feared that gore would be shed when one of the students started work, but I soon realized that the African boy has an aptitude (no doubt inherited) for using a tool in this manner. Very rapidly the object is hewed out with this tool, and I was most impressed by the way it was handled and the amount of finish that could be achieved in the hands of an experienced craftsman. You have to think of the work being aimed at, so to speak, with one hand.

The next stage is performed with smaller tools, shaped something like adzes. The English name the Africans give to these tools is 'hoes', and that is quite a good one for a general description. They use flat ones with an edge like our chisels, and round ones like our gouges—a large and small one of each. Here again the work has to be aimed at with one hand while it is held firmly with the other. A good many boys use either hand according to convenience. The object now has assumed a very definite shape, and in old experienced hands is almost finished. A large knife, or small one if the work is small, is employed now for smoothing the work and giving precision to edges and angles, and engraving patterns, &c., on the surface. To do this the craftsman takes the carving *in* his hand and holds it firmly on his knees, or against his chest maybe, and works, in the case of smoothing, the tool away from his body. They use also rasps and files and even sandpaper for final finish. In the bush they use a rough leaf for this purpose, as our old medieval craftsmen employed the skin of a certain fish. Personally I like them to get their finish with the carving tools where possible.

After the demonstration lesson by the master, I had the class arranged in a circle all squatting on their blocks with chopping-block in front and their piece of wood. The master sat in the middle, also squatting on a low block on which he could turn easily to give instruction and advice. As a rule the boys are quite definite as to what they wish to carve; but I find it often necessary to advise them to do something else. Their imagination prompts them to impossible tasks—like the carving of a model of a motor-car or bicycle. To boys all the world over such things appeal.

The boys quickly got to work and soon I had a collection of carvings, little and big, of extraordinary interest, my difficulty being to house them all. There are about two hundred boys (including some girls) carving. Apart from the impossible objects mentioned above, the students' work was happily chosen. I encouraged them to look for models in their own land; native objects that they knew about and could visualize without unduly straining their little brains. When they realized how interesting these were to carve, they gave up, to a great extent, wanting to turn out aeroplanes, &c. Models of State swords are a favourite—and are excellent practice in the actual carving—not being too difficult and being beautiful objects in themselves. Chiefs' stools, with their various interesting patterns and symbolic devices, were attacked with vigour and we have some very good models of these. Native household implements—foofoo mortars and pestles, spoons (some beautiful designs), knives, drinking cups, vases, and wands of office. Like all boys they love carving animals, and soon we had a collection of animals that Noah might have envied: elephants, tortoises, birds of various sorts, snails, &c., were attempted with varying success; carved with a *naïveté* and simplicity of form which are really delightful.

The African has a good sense of form and a natural taste for design, where this has not been spoilt by injudicious teaching, and in carving they find a natural outlet for this; and theirs is an acquisitive sort of mind which quickly degenerates into mere unintelligent copying of undesirable objects of which the shops, &c., in Accra are filled—the kind of stuff that is turned out by the worst European taste. And I find an important—perhaps the most important—duty imposed on me is to persuade them of the beauty and desirableness of their own native forms.

I went recently to a village in the interior, where the official carver of stools to the Ashanti Chief has his workshops, and there saw him and his assistants at work carving a great variety of stools with their various symbolic patterns and emblematic forms. All the tools were made by the village blacksmith near by: much the same type as those mentioned above, but of a greater range and variety—beautiful. One tool of iron curved at each end (no wooden handle) was used like our spoke-shave, a large knife for planing; and a lovely axe, which they use for the first roughing out—the metal let into the wood, instead of the usual method. The dexterity with which these tools were used was very beautiful to behold. I am getting this blacksmith to make several of these tools for the carving classes at Achimota.

DESCRIPTION OF PLATES

By RICHARD CARLINE

EXPLANATORY NOTE REGARDING THE DESCRIPTION
OF PLATES

THE description is arranged so as to treat separately each of the specimens reproduced in the Plates, and for the sake of convenience the method adopted for the
first specimen illustrated in Plate I is maintained similarly for each specimen in the
succeeding plates. The order used is as follows: The first paragraph indicates
the subject which the specimen represents; the second paragraph, the materials employed, also the measurements in inches; the third paragraph, the provenance given,
if any, with the specimen, as in a label; the fourth paragraph, the probable provenance in the opinion of the writer, if differing from that indicated in the previous
paragraph, with name of the tribe, if possible, as distinct from the present purely
political area; the fifth paragraph, the name of the collection where the specimen
belongs at the time of writing, also the date when it was acquired, and also name of
the explorer or other means, if known, by which it was obtained in Africa. The
remaining paragraphs are intended as a commentary based on available information
regarding the purpose or use of the specimen, being, in the opinion of the writer,
relevant as well as helpful to the aesthetic appreciation of the West African artist's
work.

The measurements are given by means of abbreviations in the following manner:
H = height, L = length, W = width, D = depth from front to back, Diam.=
diameter.

In some of the plates an attempt has been made to show the subject of the
photograph in surroundings appropriate to it or emphasizing the utilitarian and
functional aims of West African figures, masks, as well as implements. For this
purpose minor objects which are not necessarily West African are introduced in
the background or elsewhere, and mention of them in these descriptions is accord-
ingly omitted.

In addition to the acknowledgements already given in the foreword, the writer
owes thanks to the Royal Anthropological Institute for allowing him to use their
library, also to his brother the late G. R. Carline (then Keeper of Bankfield Museum)
for his care in revising and verifying most of these descriptions.

LIST OF PLATES

I. THE RECEPTION — Carved group in wood, painted — Lagos, Nigeria (Egba-Yoruba tribe)

II. THE DRUMMER and another figure — Carved in wood, painted — Loango, B. Congo (Bavili (?) tribe)

III. THE LISTENER — Another view of seated figure in Plate II

IV. GODDESS AND CHILD — Wood, painted — Lagos, Nigeria (Egba-Yoruba tribe)

V. GODDESS AND CHILD — Another view of figure in Plate IV

VI. BEARDED MAN — Carved in wood — Ivory Coast (Baoule (?) tribe)

VII. WOMAN WITH BOWL — Carved in wood — B. Congo (Ba-Luba tribe)

VIII. MOTHER SEATED with children — Carved in wood — N. Nigeria (Yoruba tribe)

IX. ANCESTOR FIGURE and two others with offering bowls — Wood, copper-sheeted — Gabun (Bakota (?) tribe) — Carved in wood — Nigeria (Yoruba tribe) — Carved in wood — B. Congo (Ba-Luba tribe)

X. WOMAN SUPPORTING STOOL — Carved in wood — B. Congo (Maniema tribe)

XI. A WHITE MAN VISITS A CHIEF — Panelled door in wood, painted — Nigeria (Yoruba tribe)

XII. A CHIEF WITH HIS WIVES — Red earthenware — Gold Coast (Fanti (?) tribe)

XIII. THREE-FACED MASK — Wood covered with skin, decorated with paint, metal eyes — Cross River, Cameroon (Ekoi (?) tribe)

XIV. APRONED WOMAN; MAN IN CAP; MAN WITH DRESSED HAIR — Carved in wood — Sierra Leone (Mendi tribe) — " " " — Gabun (?) — " " " — Gabun (?)

XV. WOMAN'S HEAD — Mask carved in wood — Ivory Coast (Baoule (?) tribe)

XVI. WOMEN ANCESTORS — Masks in painted wood — Lagos, Nigeria (Egba-Yoruba tribe)

XVII. CRESTED HEAD and TWO-FACED HORNED HEAD — Masks carved in wood and covered with skin, metal eyes — Cross River, Nigeria (Ekoi (?) tribe)

E

LIST OF PLATES

XVIII.	BOY'S INITIATION MASK WITH PLAITED HAIR	Carved in wood, fibre coils	B. Congo (Ba-Pende tribe)
XIX.	GHOST MASK OF WOMAN	Painted wood	Gabun (Ashira (?) tribe)
XX.	WHITE MASK WITH SCARLET EYES	Ghost mask in painted wood, with eyes encircled by scarlet seeds	S. Nigeria (Ibo (?) tribe)
XXI.	WHITE MASK WITH SCARLET EYES (another view)	See XX above	
XXII.	WATER-POT with a frieze in relief (snakes devouring frogs)	Black glazed earthenware	Gold Coast (Ashanti tribe)
XXIII.	LIDDED VESSEL for ceremonial use with symbolic figures in high relief	Painted earthenware	Dahomey
XXIV.	TWO STOOLS	Light wood Blackened wood	Gold Coast (Ashanti tribe)
XXV.	GOURDS		,, ,, ,, ,, Angola (Kongo (?) tribe) Fernando Po (Bubi tribe) Nigeria (Efik (?) tribe) Sierra Leone (Mendi tribe) Gold Coast (Fanti (?) tribe) S. Africa (?)
	BASKET TRAY		Angola (Bihe tribe)
XXVI.	MUSICAL INSTRUMENTS	Harps, Harp-guitar	See Plates XXVII, XXVIII
		Fiddle with gourd resonator	B. Congo (Basonge tribe)
		War gong (iron)	N. Nigeria (Guari tribe)
		Drum	S. Nigeria (?)
XXVII.	HARPS	Another view, see Plate XXVI	Gabun (Commi (?) tribe) Gabun (Bakalai (?) tribe)
XXVIII.	HEAD OF HARP GUITAR	Another view, see Plate XXVI	Gabun (Chekiani (?) tribe)
XXIX.	CEREMONIAL HOE	Wood with iron blade	B. Congo (Ba-Kongo tribe)
	HEAD-RESTS	Carved in wood	B. Congo (N. Ba-Mbala tribe) Angola (Zombo tribe)
	RITUAL BOWL, supported on a woman's uplifted hands	,, ,, ,, Carved in wood	Dahomey
XXX.	CEREMONIAL PADDLE CANOE PADDLES	Painted wood Painted wood Plain wood Plain wood	S. Nigeria (Kalabari tribe) S. Nigeria (Jekri tribe) S. Nigeria (Sobo tribe) Angola (Mussorongo (?) tribe)

26

	HOE	Wood with blade of iron	Gambia (Mandingo tribe)
XXXI.	GOLD WEIGHTS	Brass cast by process of *cire perdue*	Gold Coast (Ashanti tribe)
	SPOON FOR LIFTING GOLD DUST	Beaten brass	,, ,, ,,
	BOX FOR STORING GOLD DUST	Brass-casting	,, ,, ,,
	FINGER RINGS	Brass-casting	,, ,, ,,
XXXII.	WINE VESSEL	Incised earthenware	B. Congo (Mangbettu tribe)
	LAMP	Perforated earthenware	N. Gold Coast (Fra-fra tribe)
	TOBACCO BOX (in form of a bird)	Carved in wood	Nigeria (Borgo tribe)
	PIPE (with bowl in shape of elephant's head)	Brass-casting, wood, beads	Cameroon (Bamoum tribe)
	WATER-PIPE	Gourd decorated with copper, and earthenware	Northern Rhodesia (Awemba tribe)

PLATE I

THE RECEPTION

Group of figures representing a white man on horseback, surrounded by native attendants, musicians, and women, upon a round base which rests on the heads of another group of figures representing a native chief on horseback with armed attendants, standing on a circular base.

Soft wood; painted; H. (whole) 32″, (horseman) 15″; Diam. 14″.
Stated to be 'from Yoruba'.
Probably Egba (Yoruba) tribe, Lagos, Nigeria.
Brighton Public Museum, before 1890.

The group is dominated by the figure of a bearded European, and the subject represents his reception at a native village with accompaniment of music, parading of guns, and domestic scenes. All the figures are painted. The period is probably about mid-nineteenth century judging by the appearance of the 'white man's' pointed black beard and large hat. The visitor is riding on a horse and holds the reins in his left hand, and a large revolver in his right. His coat is painted white with black spots and his trousers greyish-blue with venetian-red stripes and spots; the flesh is pink-coloured. A figure of a nude female, painted blue (ultramarine), is shown astride the rump of the horse, partly sitting on her left heel, and with the right leg outstretched behind; in her right hand she holds a staff, which is also held by another female figure.

The figure on the right of the horseman represents an attendant carrying a folded umbrella in the left hand; his hair is shaven except for three circular patches, depicting a form of hair dressing said to be commonly worn by the Mohammedan Hausas.

Besides this figure, two others also represent men, wearing shirts decorated with broad vertical bands painted alternately salmon-pink and either bluish-grey, white, or blue. Both the latter figures are musicians, wearing caps resembling the cloth type worn by men among the Yoruba; they carry arm-drums, painted black and white, suspended by blue shoulder-straps, and hold beaters in the right hand. The four figures representing women are shown with the hair elaborately dressed, depicting a Yoruba style said to be worn by married women; two of them wear skirts, and one of them carries three rattles (?). The colour of the flesh varies in each figure, from red (venetian) to yellow (ochre), that of the nude standing figure being salmon-pink; the facial marks, in the form of gashes, are painted blue (ultramarine).

The rim of the base, on which the figures stand, is painted red (venetian) and is decorated with a row of seven figures in relief representing nude females, painted alternately salmon-pink, blue, white, yellow (ochre).

On the lower tier, in the centre, is another mounted figure representing a native chief as the host, wearing a hat resembling a night-cap; a spear or staff is held in his right hand, and the reins in his left hand. As on the tier above, a nude female, painted blue, is seated astride on the rump of the horse, but is facing backwards; she holds aloft, horizontally, another nude female, possibly a child, painted red (venetian), whose hair is shaven like the child suckled on the upper tier. They are surrounded by six soldiers all facing in the same direction, and carrying guns. None of these figures, however, are visible in the plate.

In the space between their heads and the under surface of the upper tier is a row of figures representing alternately the mud-fish, painted black, and the porcupine, which is painted alternately yellow ochre and salmon-pink, lying on its back.

The form of the carving is based on that of a stool, though obviously not meant for practical use, having figures on the seat. It is a characteristic product of a 'school' of carving, as it might be termed, which belongs to the coastal region of Porto Novo and Lagos, and dates probably from relatively recent times, namely since 1750, when the Yoruba State expanded to include this region.[1] The style is partly derived from the influence of Benin which preceded that of the Yoruba at Lagos.[1] The polychrome painting, and subjects based on lively scenes of natural life, may be the Yoruba contribution; whereas the hard, precise, and rather literal manner may be that of Benin.

PLATE II
DRUMMER AND ANOTHER FIGURE

Figure of a man standing on a large base, beating a drum with his hands.

Soft wood; painted; H. 29"; W. (shoulders) 9"; D. (base) 11".
Stated to be 'from Congo'.
Probably Mayombe or Bavili tribes, Loango, Belgian Congo.
Cambridge University Museum, 1911. (Forfeitt Collection.)

There are traces of white paint on the figure, indicating that the face and neck were probably painted; other portions of the figure are thinly painted black, namely eyes, upper part of body, rear end of drum, and pattern on base; the rest of it remains the natural colour of the wood (light yellow ochre).

[1] P. A. Talbot, *Southern Nigeria*, vol. i.

The teeth of the figure are depicted chipped or filed to a point, in accordance with the custom[1] among the lower Congo tribes. The cone-shaped head-dress appears to be a cap with a tassel at the top. Caps were worn as a badge of sovereignty or nobility among the tribes subject to the old Kingdom of Kongo. At the Kakongo coronation, which Dennett[2] attended, in 1891, the effigy of the late Neamlau (King) 'was wearing his native cap (made of the fibre of the pine-apple) with the name Neamlau marked on it'; and as this cap was the emblem of sovereignty, the Neamlau-elect had to content himself meanwhile by wearing a 'military helmet with a white plume, marked "10th Prince Albert's Own" '. H. U. Hall[3] quotes the observation of Barbot in the Kingdom of Kongo in the seventeenth century: 'The King commonly wears a white cap on his head; as do the nobility that are in favour; and this is so eminent a token thereof, that if he is displeased at any of them, he only causes his cap to be taken off from his head; for that white cap is a cognisance of nobility there.'

Possibly the black painted upper portion of the figure is intended to depict the close-fitting black jacket of European make, generally worn, like the cap, by persons of rank, sometimes with no other garment. Judging by the dress, therefore, the figure is perhaps intended for a person of rank such as a drummer attached to the court.

The bangle depicted round the left wrist corresponds with Dennett's[4] description of the copper bracelet called *lembe*, worn among the Bavili, to signify marriage by a certain rite.

The fingers of both hands are in contact with the drum. The latter tapers to its base, length 13″, and has a ridge-like projection as handle (?) in the middle of the upper side, resembling a drum 113″ long, in the Horniman Museum,[5] with two ridges, apparently handles, one in the form of a long-tailed animal. This type of drum belongs to the Maritime and Cataract regions of the Congo.[6] Among the Bavili[7] it is used for beating messages, being called *nkonko*, and is formed from a log of wood some 6 feet long. R. E. Dennett[7] records a personal experience of its utility: 'In 1881, we in Landana heard of the wreck of the mail steamer "Ethiopia", sixty or seventy miles away, one or two hours after its actual occurrence, in Luango, by drum message.'

[1] R. E. Dennett, *At the Back of the Black Man's Mind*, London, 1906, p. 76; Sir H. Johnston, *George Grenfell and the Congo*, vol. ii, p. 571.

[2] Op. cit., pp. 17, 19.

[3] *The Museum Journal*, Philadelphia, March 1923, p. 56.

[4] Op. cit., p. 11.

[5] Described, on an old label, 'from Dahomey', but perhaps not authoritatively.

[6] Cf. illustrations in *Annales du Musée du Congo belge*.

[7] Op. cit., pp. 76, 77.

Presumably, therefore, the figure represents a court drummer tapping a telegraphic signal.

The provenance of the figure is not recorded, but the region is indicated by the collector's name, Forfeitt. This presumably denotes one of the brothers of that name of the Baptist Missionary Society, and probably, as in the case of Plate III, the Rev. Lawson Forfeitt who, according to information given by the B.M.S., resided after 1889 chiefly at their mission station at Underhill, close to Matadi. If the figure was received there, its tribal provenance would be either the Kongo tribe south of the river, or the Mayombe north of it. The latter tribe are the close neighbours of the Bavili, the two tribes forming, as regards figure-carving, practically one 'school'.

That the figure belongs to this 'school' is corroborated by comparison with other examples, which are generally designated in public collections by the terms 'Loango', 'Bavili', or 'Mayombe', if designated at all. The similarities are less apparent in the treatment of the head as in the rest of the figure. They are most marked in the straight legs—comparatively long for West African art—without bend at the knee, the broad flat feet firmly planted, and the attitude of leaning forward as if over balanced, and lastly the feeling of sensuousness with which the surface is carved and the fingers and toes separately modelled.

Large bowl. (Shown base uppermost in background of photograph.)

Gourd; H. 8"; Diam. 16¾", 17¼".

Probably from Lokoja or Zungeroo, Nupe Province, Nigeria.

Halifax, Bankfield Museum, 1927. (Collected by Nurse M. Farrow about 1904.) The bowl is formed from the half section of a very large gourd, ½" thick, and is painted, on the outside, dark pink with black bands. It is also decorated with incised lines, varying in thickness; and, on the inside, with a pattern of lines formed by burning.

PLATE III

THE LISTENER

(*Another view of seated figure in Plate II*)

Figure of a seated man on a circular base.

Soft wood; painted; H. 20"; Diam. (base) 7½".

Stated to be 'from Congo'.

Probably Mayombe or Bavili tribes, Loango, Belgian Congo.

Cambridge University Museum, 1908. (Collected by Rev. L. Forfeitt, B.M.S.) This figure is thinly painted, with the exception of the base, which remains the natural colour of the wood (light yellow ochre); the hair, skirt, and seat are black, the remainder white. A necklace of beads round the neck consists of small sections of brown cane.

The head-dress, resembling a mitre, concave at the front and convex at the back, probably depicts a form of hair-dressing;[1] and the teeth, as in Plate II, are shown partially filed or chipped.

The figure is depicted wearing a skirt with fringe at the bottom, a waist belt, and bangles and anklets. The costume probably resembles that described by Dennett[2] regarding a coronation procession, in which the people 'were all dressed in cloths dyed red, and each wore a heavy silver leg ring about his ankle; the contrast between the dull red cloth and the bright metal was striking'.

The right hand of the figure is shown resting on a circular box-shaped object with projection in front, placed on the right knee; the left hand (broken off) was presumably similarly placed. It is difficult to identify this object. Though it does not resemble a drum, nevertheless any object which can be tapped is often used as such for making sound. On the other hand it may possibly depict the 'small but neatly made basket of grass with tight-fitting lid on it', described by Dennett,[3] used by the priest as a means of arbitration in disputes; 'When the name of the guilty one is mentioned he finds it impossible to take this lid off.'

The circular seat resembles a log of wood, but is perhaps meant to depict a barrel.[4]

The name of the collector of this figure indicates that its provenance is the same region as the preceding figure. The two figures, however, differ in style of carving, chiefly as regards the head. That of this figure (shown in detail) bears a close resemblance—more so than that of the preceding figure—to other Bavili wood carvings (assuming the designations usually given), features which may be enumerated namely the curved lips, open mouth, delicate nose, arched brows, wide cheekbones, and chiefly the long neck leaning forward with a tilt upwards of the head. These appear to be the characteristics of what may be described as the Bavili 'school'.

Possibly the character of the head is based on the features of the Bavili royal line, for it bears a remarkable resemblance to that of their old king-elect, Maniluemba, judging by a photograph which reveals, according to Dennett,[5] his 'rather fine Jewish cast of face'.

[1] Cf. a similar example described as a coiffure and ascribed to 'Mayumbe'; E. Torday and T. A. Joyce, *Annales du Musée du Congo belge*, Série III, vol. i, Brussels, 1902–6, Fig. 431.

[2] Op. cit., p. 20.
[3] Op. cit., p. 28.
[4] Cf. some figures in the British Museum.
[5] Op. cit., pp. 10, 11.

PLATE IV

GODDESS AND CHILD

Large figure of a woman seated upon a stool with a male attendant and a dog, and holding a fan and a child on her knee. (Also shown in Plate V.)

Wood; painted; H. 31"; W. (base) 16¼"; D. (base) 12".

Stated to be 'from Lagos'.

Probably Egba (Yoruba) tribe, Lagos, Nigeria.

Horniman Museum. (Collected by Major-General Sir A. Crofton Atkins, 1896.)

The subject of this group is probably the Yoruba deity, Odudua, in the role of mother-goddess of the earth. One of the chief temples of this goddess is at Ado,[1] north-west of Lagos, and this carving may have originally belonged there.

The group is carved from one block of wood which is light orange in colour. Parts of it are painted, and probably the whole was originally so, the colours being black, white, red (scarlet vermilion), and blue (cobalt); the parts painted black are the hair, pupils of the eyes, marks on the forehead, and the base and dog, the parts painted white being the eyes, shoulder ornament, fan, and figures of child and attendant; the blue is confined to the eyelids and marks on the face, in accordance with the use of native antimony in that manner; the vermilion remains only in faint traces on face and body.

The treatment of the hair represents a fashion adopted by Yoruba women when married in which the hair is gathered together in a central crest, and contrasts with that of the child which is largely shaven. The marks on the face in the form of lozenge-shaped gashes in groups of three depict a form of cicatrization of the skin worn by the Egba.[2] According to Talbot these are usually made 'about the same time as circumcision',[3] which explains why the infant child does not have them. But the triple vertical marks (called *pele*) shown on the child's cheeks denote that Mohammedanism was included among the faiths of its supposed parents.[3]

Both figures wear bangles round their wrists, and the mother wears also a necklace; the carved rod, painted red, blue, and white, which rests across her breasts is probably an insignia of rank.[4] The fan, which she holds in the right hand, has a similar significance; its circular shape shows it to be intended for the type made of cowhide.[5] Its handle is supported on the head of an attendant who stands on one side of the base (shown in Plate V); he is depicted wearing a cap with ear flaps,

[1] P. A. Talbot, *Southern Nigeria*, vol. ii, p. 30.

[2] R. F. Burton, *A visit to Abeokuta.*

[3] *Southern Nigeria*, vol. iii, p. 397.

[4] Cf. similar objects on some figures in the British Museum.

[5] Cf. Pl. XXXII.

short trousers, and carrying a drum slung over the left shoulder on which he plays with both hands.

The stool on which the woman sits is cylindrical in shape representing the simple form of stool in ordinary use.

The dog is shown seated on its haunches and wearing a collar round its neck. It is an animal sacred to Ogun,[1] god of war and iron, for which reason its head is found in every blacksmith's shop. The god is reputed to be the grandchild of Odudua, which serves to explain the inclusion of the dog in this family group of divinities, somewhat like, and perhaps even derived from, the ancient Egyptian conception of Isis and Horus.

The group belongs to the same 'school' of wood-carving as that shown in Plate I, and is an unusually large and probably important example.

Woven cloth (left background in photograph).

Cotton and silk; L. 92″; W. 63″.
Stated to be 'from Warri district'.
Probably Jekri tribe, South Nigeria.
Halifax, Bankfield Museum. (Probably collected by Dr. F. N. Roth.)

This cloth was probably woven on the 'continuous warp' loom, generally used by women,[2] but is exceptional in length and consists of four strips joined in the width. The pattern, which is of silk, appears on one side only, formed by the method known as 'floating', the colours being bright green (emerald) and red-violet, in small alternate squares; the borders at each end are of the latter colour with narrow blue stripes.

It was probably collected when Dr. F. N. Roth was in Southern Nigeria in the early nineties.

PLATE V
GODDESS AND CHILD
(*Another view of figure in Plate IV*)

Woman seated upon a stool, with a male attendant and a dog, and holding a fan and a child on her knee. (See Plate IV.)

Woven cloth (background in photograph, also shown in Plate VIII).

Cotton; L. 69″; W. 38″.
Stated to be 'from Opobo'.
Probably Ibo tribe, South Nigeria.
Liverpool Free Public Museum, 1901.

[1] P. A. Talbot, *Southern Nigeria*, vol. ii, p. 88.

[2] G. R. Carline, *The Horizontal Narrow-band Loom in Africa*, B.A. Paper, S. Africa, 1929.

The width indicates the cloth was woven on the 'continuous warp' loom which enables the warp threads, when cut, to be tied into tassels at each end.[1]

The colour used in the warp is creamy-white, and also red (venetian) in narrow lines down the sides. The colours used in the weft are red (venetian), pale yellow, green, and black, none of which appear on the reverse side owing to the use of the process known as 'floating'. The design consists of eight horizontal bands of black and white check or of red diamonds with black centres. In Plate VIII is shown another of the three cloths stated to have been woven on the same loom as this specimen.

This type of cloth is woven by the Ibo tribe, according to P. A. Talbot,[2] and is 'called *akwete*, but formerly termed *akwa-miri* (cloth of the water) because it was originally said to have been made for use as a towel when bathing'; it is worn for occasions of ceremony. The same author also informs us that these cloths are little made nowadays 'owing to the great expansion in the imports of Manchester goods'.[3] Furthermore, European cottons and dyes are used 'which run in the wash, whereas pieces woven thirty years ago from native products are as fresh to-day as when they came from the loom'.[2]

PLATE VI
BEARDED MAN

Figure of a bearded man.

> Soft wood; H. 21½"; W. 4⅞"; D. 5½".
> Stated to be 'from Lahou, Ivory Coast'.
> Probably Baoule or Guerret tribes.
> *Bristol Museum*, 1914.

The wood is light in colour, but is thinly painted black. The figure has neat, delicate designs carved in relief on face, front of body, neck, and back, depicting cicatrices of the skin in a style usual in Ivory Coast figures. The hair, in the form of a high ridge, represents a form of a hair-dressing characteristic of Ivory Coast tribes. The hair is brushed upwards into a central crest, with the ends tied along its centre. The edges are neatly sewn all round, often in a broad band behind the ear, as depicted in this figure. This form of hair-dressing is often combined with the wearing of beard or whiskers, which are divided into a series of points.[4]

The figure stands on a rectangular base which is decorated similarly back and front but differently each side.

[1] G. R. Carline, op. cit.
[2] *Tribes of the Niger Delta*, 1932, p. 278.
[3] *Southern Nigeria*, vol. iii, p. 941.
[4] Cf. Photographs from the Guerret tribe, Ivory Coast (Series G. Lerat, Exposition Coloniale, Paris, 1931). See also Pl. XV.

That the figure belongs to the region of the Ivory Coast is demonstrated by comparison with other figures[1] so labelled, which similarly display the drooping eyelids, the long flat nose, small but protruding mouth, hollow cheeks, combined with rounded legs and large but very flat feet, with a similar feeling of meditation, reserve, and dignity. In treatment of the face there are superficial similarities to the less formulated figure-carvings of the neighbouring Ashanti, suggesting that the provenance of this figure is either the Baoule tribe who are said[2] to belong to the Agni-Ashanti group, or their neighbours the Guerret. The traditions of this 'school' probably evolved early.

Cloth mat (bottom of photograph).

> Cotton; L. 20½"; W. 14".
> Stated to be 'from Lahou, Ivory Coast'.
> Probably Baoule tribe.
> *Bristol Museum*, 1914.

The mat consists of four strips woven on the narrow-band loom and sewn together, a method of weaving confined to the horizontal type of loom used by men, which, spreading with the cultivation of cotton, superseded the older woman's loom.[3]

The colours used in the warp are bluish-black and white, with deep crimson down one side. The same colours are in the weft; the patterns, formed with black, being as follows: first band (to the right in the plate), white only; second band, crimson only; third band, white only; and fourth, alternately crimson and white.

PLATE VII

WOMAN WITH BOWL

Figure of a woman seated on the ground and holding a wooden bowl in front of her (also shown in Plate IX).

> Wood; H. 20"; W. (head) 6"; D. 7".
> Stated to be Ba-Luba tribe, Belgian Congo.
> *British Museum*, 1905.

The figure and bowl are carved from a single piece of light-coloured wood which is thinly painted black.

The figure is depicted unclothed except in so far as the elaborate decoration on the front of the body, extending round the waist to the back, depicting cicatrices or

---

[1] Cf. H. Clouzot and A. Level, *L'Art nègre*, Pl. xxxvii.

[2] *La Côte d'Ivoire*, Pub. Gouvernement-Général de l'Afrique Française, 1906, p. 468.

[3] G. R. Carline, op. cit.; and *Primitive Weaving*, B.A. Paper, Leeds, 1927.

raised lumps in the skin, serves as a substitute for dress. The design consists of rows of small lozenges with a few larger long ones, with the navel as its central pivot, and resembles the style worn by the Ba-Luba people.

A row of three small cicatrices are also shown in front of each ear, a decoration sometimes depicted in Ba-Luba figure-carvings, generally of the northerly Urua (Warua) region.[1]

The treatment of the hair (cf. Plate X) represents the Ba-Luba mode of hair-dressing worn by men and women alike, and consists of a bunch at the back with a frontal band above the forehead; the latter is probably formed with finely plaited hair.[2] There are two modes, according to E. Torday,[3] in which Ba-Luba hair-dressing is constructed, one by which the hair is drawn over a circular wooden ring at the back of the head and the other—practised in the more southerly region—in which they 'weave their hair with the aid of basket work into a kind of halo decked with beads and cowries by way of jewellery'. It is difficult to identify which of these modes is depicted in this figure; both probably resemble one another being augmented with false hair, oil, grease, and powder.

The small projections at the back of the hair probably depict the lancets used in the cicatrization of the skin, and also used as hairpins in this manner.[4]

The bowl is probably intended to represent the ordinary household wooden food bowl and has a cross-hatch band of decoration round the rim, which closely resembles that carved on a porridge bowl of the Katanga region.[5]

The subject of this carving, namely the empty bowl held in the lap of a woman, is frequently depicted in Ba-Luba figure-carving; examples are variously ascribed to the Urua (Warua),[6] Maniema,[7] and Kayumba.[8] Of these regions of Ba-Luba territory, the last named in the neighbourhood of the Lualaba river is the most likely provenance of this figure, judging by the resemblance of the pattern carved on the bowl to the Katanga specimen mentioned above and its dissimilarity to those shown in Urua work.

The Maniema specimen[7], which is of quite different style of carving,[9] is described

[1] Cf. a Mask (Urua tribe) in Linden Museum, Stuttgart (E. Wasmuth, 'Masken', *Orbis Pictus*, 13, p. 14), and another in Berlin Museum (E. von Sydow, *Die Kunst der Naturvölker*, p. 141).

[2] H. U. Hall (quoting Hein and Stanley), *The Museum Journal*, Philadelphia, Sept. 1923, p. 192.

[3] *Women of all Nations*, p. 320.

[4] V. L. Cameron, *J.R.A.I.*, vol. vi, p. 169; and *Across Africa*, 1877, pp. 303, 304.

[5] In Brighton Public Museum.

[6] Philadelphia Museum (*The Museum Journal*, June 1923, Fig. 26).

[7] Congo Museum, Tervueren, Belgium (J. Maes and H. Lavachery, *L'Art nègre*, Brussels, 1930, Pl. 21).

[8] Ibid. (*Annales du Musée du Congo*, Série III, Brussels, 1902–6, Pl. xlviii).

[9] Cf. stool figure, Pl. X.

as representing a figure of a mendicant ('figurine mendiante'). It is not clear whether the description is authentic or a surmise based on its resemblance to the stereotyped conception of a beggar in bowed and kneeling attitude with doleful expression and emaciated limbs; as shown in Plate X, it is an aspect characteristic of the Maniema carvings of the human figure. Such an interpretation is scarcely applicable in the case of our statue, with its cheerful expression and sprightly attitude. More probably the figure is intended to portray the ordinary attitude of a Ba-Luba woman engaged in the household task of preparing a dish of manioc while seated on the mud floor inside or outside her hut.

Probably the function of the figure is a purely religious one and the 'mendicant' interpretation should be applied to its use rather than its subject; namely that the empty bowl is intended for the reception of offerings, not begged for but given in the form of payment, in connexion with some form of religious consultation.

PLATE VIII

MOTHER SEATED WITH CHILDREN[1]

Large figure of a woman seated on a stool with an infant girl on her lap, an infant boy on her back, and a bigger boy sitting on her shoulders.

Hard wood; H. 27"; W. (shoulders) 10½"; D. (base) 11½".
Stated to be 'Yoruba of the Benue River district'.
Northern Yoruba tribe, Nigeria.
Horniman Museum, 1929. (Collected by Major F. H. Ruxton.)

The subject of this group is probably the earth-mother goddess Odudua as of Plates IV and V. It is part of a collection stated to have been made among the Munshi, Fulani, and other tribes of the Benue River area, Northern Nigeria.

The wood is thinly painted black; and the whole group is carved from one piece, with the exception of the baby lying on the mother's lap, its two arms, and the head of the child clinging to her back, which are separate pieces fitted on with pegs; the last mentioned can be turned to face either side. There are necklaces of small metal beads round the neck of the woman and bigger child, and small tassels of crimson silk in her ears.

The figure of the woman is depicted nude, except for several bands which encircle the waist at the back only, probably representing rings of metal. Her hands are shown resting on her knees, with the figure of the child lying across them; the left hand of the child is shown holding the mother's left breast; its right arm is missing.

[1] The figure and the cloths shown in the background are described in Plates IX and V.

The hair is depicted by means of incised lines, that of the woman being formed into a central crest. The faces have diagonal grooves depicting skin cicatrices, which are also represented by rectangular patterns incised on arms and body.

Apart from the treatment of the faces, the carving closely resembles that of the semi-Sudanese tribes of the Upper Niger and Upper Volta Rivers of French West Africa,[1] namely the thin long neck, elongated bodies and limbs, square shoulders, large pendant breasts, and firm solid feet as well as its black surface and the feeling it gives of definition and weight. On the other hand, the carving of the faces is northern Yoruba, the treatment in a pliable and almost florid manner being characteristic of the northern group of that people as quite distinct from that of the Lagos style shown in Plates I, IV, V.

Though the group is said to have been collected in the region of the Benue River, one cannot fail to see the influence, if not the work, of the craftsmen of the more northern tribes dwelling on the Upper Niger.

PLATE IX

ANCESTOR FIGURE AND TWO OTHERS WITH OFFERING BOWLS

Ancestor guardian figure (centre in the Plate).

> Wood and copper; H. 23"; W. 12"; D. 2".
> Stated to be 'from Ogowai region, Gabun'.
> Probably Bakota tribe.
> *British Museum*, 1922. (Formerly in the Collection of Captain A. W. F. Fuller.)

The figure is carved from one piece of dark-coloured wood, the front surface of which is entirely covered with metal sheets. The metal used in this case is copper, but comparison with other figures of similar type show that brass is generally used also.[2]

In general form and design it is similar to other examples of this type, namely a concave face surrounded by flat pieces with two small pendants and with a piece shaped like a crescent moon above it. The treatment is stylized, but it represents a person's head, surrounded, apparently, with elaborate hair dressing. Assuming the latter surmise to be correct, the shapes surrounding the face would be obtained by depicting a side view of the person's coiffure, as if turned to face the front in one plane. The head would thus have to be regarded three—dimensionally, by viewing the upper piece as a central crest extending backwards along the head, and the

---

[1] Cf. a seated female figure with similar waist rings and patterns on arms and breast, reproduced in *Vision and Design* (Roger Fry), probably from the Upper Niger, though its provenance is not stated, other than the description 'Negro Art'.

[2] Cf. examples in the British Museum and the Bristol Museum.

other pieces as if they were the sides of the coiffure with projections downwards; an arrangement like this resembles the fashion in hairdressing most prevalent among the tribes of the Ogowai region.

There are some examples[1] of this type of figure in which the head is much smaller relatively to the rest, a type which is much rarer, and possibly an older form.

The figure is probably not an object of direct worship itself. Its function is guardianship of the ancestor's bones. The latter are placed in baskets into the midst of which the base of the figure is inserted.[2]

Determination of the provenance of the figure is complicated by the fact that ancestor veneration is not a cult confined to any single tribe, but is a feature of religion throughout the Gabun.[3] The provenance most frequently named for such figures is a very generalized one, namely the Ogowai River.[4] A series from the Trocadero Museum, Paris, reproduced by L. Frobenius[5] (and described as masks!) are stated to be from Ondumbo ('Ndumbo?) on the south side of the river. On the other hand, another example in the British Museum is ascribed to the Bakota, who occupy a neighbouring region on the north bank. The latter is the most likely provenance, being nearer the territory of the Fan who have customs closely resembling that involved in this figure.

[For description of Woman with Bowl, on left of this photograph, see Plate VII.]

Figure of a kneeling woman holding a basket in front of her. (Also shown in Pl. VIII, background.)

> Soft wood; painted; H. 19″; Diam. (base) 5½″.
> No recorded provenance.
> Probably northern Yoruba tribe, Nigeria.
> *Imperial Institute.* (Presented by the Government of Northern Nigeria, 1910.)

The figure is carved from one piece of wood and is painted the colour of deep pink, except for the hair which is black; the pink colour is probably the dye extracted from the Camwood tree. On the smooth polished parts of the figure the colour is darker, but in the crevices where the powder remains it is lighter and opaque. The colour has also been applied over the broken parts.

The figure depicts a nude woman kneeling on a circular base and sitting on her

---

[1] Musée Ethnographique, Trocadero, Paris.

[2] Cf. an example shown thus in the collection cited above.

[3] P. Du Chaillu, *Adventures in Equatorial Africa*, pp. 335, 336; A. Lang, *The Religion of the Fans.*

[4] H. Clouzot and A. Level, *L'Art nègre,* Pl. xxv.

[5] *Die Masken,* 1898, Figs. 44–8.

heels. Three lozenge-shaped gashes on each cheek depict the facial marks worn by the Egba (Yoruba)[1]; and the hair represents a style worn among the same group by married women.[1] Both these features are usually shown in carvings from that region. The figure has bangles round each wrist and a number of rings round the neck. There are also bands of herring-bone pattern finely incised on each breast.

The receptacle held with both hands in front of the waist is probably intended for a basket, judging by the pattern with which it is covered. Its function may be like that of the adjoining figure, namely to receive offerings in connexion with some religious purpose. In the Berlin Museum[2] there is from the same region a similar type of kneeling female figure holding a wooden bowl which is described as a receptacle for kola nuts. These nuts are often eaten in connexion with ceremonial functions,[3] and are kept or sent away as presents in special boxes; they are chiefly used for making vows or oaths of friendship, which may be the method of employment as regards this figure.

Despite the Egba (south Yoruba) resemblances so far noted in this figure, it does not belong in style of carving to the work of that 'school'. Its loose, free, and rather florid carving completely differs from the sharpness and precision characteristic of such examples as are shown in Plates I, IV, V. It belongs rather to the northern Yoruba 'school' of which the heads of the figures shown in Plate VIII are an example.

Cloth with check pattern.

Raphia palm; L. 191"; W. 15¼".
Bushongo tribe, Belgian Congo.
British Museum. (Collected by E. Torday, 1909.)

The cloth consists of a number of squares each separately woven and stitched together. The light ones vary in colour from that of cream to yellow-ochre, and the dark ones are purplish vandyke brown.

As regards the last-named colour, Mr. T. A. Joyce informed the writer that it is obtained by dipping the material in mud from the swamps.

PLATE X
WOMAN SUPPORTING STOOL

Stool consisting of the figure of a woman kneeling on a circular base and supporting the seat on her head and tips of her fingers.

[1] See Pl. IV.
[2] E. von Sydow, *Die Kunst der Naturvölker*, Berlin, 1923, Pl. i. Cf. also an example in the Leipzig Museum (J. Maes and H. Lavachery, *L'Art nègre*, Pl. 26) described as a figure of a mendicant.
[3] H. Ling Roth, *Great Benin*, pp. 59, 61.

Wood; H. 21″; Diam. (seat) 11″.

Stated to be 'from Manyama' (Maniema, Ba-Luba) tribe, Belgian Congo.

British Museum, 1905.

The stool is carved from a single piece of wood and is thinly painted black.[1] The figure is decorated with coloured glass trade beads in the form of strings and two square aprons, one at the front and the other at the back, of the type usually worn by the women of Maniema;[2] those round the waist and head are blue (turquoise), and those round the loins dark blue; the other strings are white.

Apart from the beads the figure is depicted nude; its kneeling attitude is one of slightly leaning forward, with neck bent, more so than appears in the photograph.

The decoration of the body, consisting of small lozenges, forms a design extending round the back with the navel as centre, and depicts cicatrices of the skin in the style worn by the Ba-Luba. The hair is also treated in a style usual in Ba-Luba carvings with an arrangement of plaits at the back similar to that on the head of the figure in Plate VII, and a band representing plaited hair over the top of the forehead. The border of this coiffure, which, seen from the back, resembles the expanding petals of a flower, appears to be a special feature of the local mode, judging by its similar rendering in other Maniema carvings. It is probably the feature which Cameron[3] likens to a coronet, and its shape probably results from the use of the 'circular wooden ring at the back of the head over which they draw the hair'.[4]

That this stool is correctly ascribed to Maniema art is demonstrated by the similarity of the figure to that of other examples[5] also given the same provenance, a similarity chiefly shown in its broad flat hands with long extended fingers, its facial features, and its emaciated and bony limbs with distended belly.

Its pronounced 'Semitic' type of face may be accounted for by the physiognomy of the Maniema people, who are said to include an admixture of Ethiopian stock.[6]

It is improbable that the head is the portrait of an actual individual, as its carving is of a type invariably copied in each example of Maniema figure carving. But the original model on which it was based was possibly an example of realistic portraiture, depicting perhaps some particular woman of rank or importance.

[1] Obtained by burying in boggy ground, according to H. von Wissmann, *From the Congo to the Zambezi* (Trans. N. J. A. Bergmann), London, 1891, p. 172.

[2] V. L. Cameron, *Across Africa*, p. 355.

[3] *J.R.A.I.*, vol. vi, p. 169.

[4] E. Torday, *Women of All Nations*, p. 320.

[5] Stool in Leipzig Museum, and bowl figure in Tervueren Museum, Belgium (J. Maes and H. Lavachery, *L'Art nègre*, Pls. 21, 27); stool with two standing figures, man and woman, in Berlin Museum (E. von Sydow, *Die Kunst der Naturvölker*, p. 145); standing stool figure collected on the Lualaba River by Wissmann, op. cit., facing p. 172. Chief Russuna's stool, ill. by Cameron, op. cit., vol. ii, p. 17.

[6] Sir H. Johnston, *George Grenfell and the Congo*, p. 52.

Its aspect of depicting old age, and its half-closed eyes resembling a state of sleep or even death, can perhaps be accounted for as the intention to represent an ancestor or ghost.

PLATE XI

A WHITE MAN VISITS A CHIEF

Door in the form of a series of panels decorated with the representation of a white man with his attendants visiting a native chief and villagers.

Wood; painted; W. 4' 2".
Stated to be 'from Ikerre, Nigeria'.
Probably Yoruba tribe.
British Museum, 1924. (Previously an exhibit at the British Empire Exhibition, Wembley, 1924.)

The door was lent to the Wembley Exhibition by the Ogoga (chief) of Ikerre, from whom it was subsequently obtained by the British Museum by means of exchange, a large high-backed chair, specially made, being given in return.

The door consists of two separate solid pieces, constructed to swing on slots in a frame. There is also a lintel, which is separate, and not shown in the photograph; it is decorated with a row of human faces being pecked by vultures.

The figures are all in bas-relief, carved out of the solid wood. In some cases they are in high relief, so nearly detached from their background as to constitute carving in the round, and the treatment as a whole corresponds to the Greek metope more than to bas-relief as usually meant.

The whole of the surface is painted; the surrounding edge is red (venetian); the ridges, forming frames round each panel, are black; the remainder is painted in various colours, mostly red and black with the addition of light blue (greenish cerulean) and light yellow (naples). The flesh is painted either red or black, and costumes either blue, red, or black.

The style is that of the Yoruba, and somewhat resembles that of the polychrome wood carvings of the Lagos district.

The panels of the left-hand side represent, apparently, the chief and native people, and those of the right-hand side their white visitor and his attendants.

The chief is shown in the large panel (on the left, second from the top), seated on a chair of the ordinary 'fold-up' camp variety, with hands placed firmly on his knees, and looking directly at his approaching visitor. His dress consists of a plain skirt (yellow) and the only evidence of rank is the tall, conical decorated hat, probably intended to depict the type of crown made with coloured beads like some in the

British Museum. He is shown supported behind by a tall, elegant female figure (red in colour), nude except for several black rings round the waist.

In the panel above are shown villagers (men) carrying domestic or farm implements. In the panel below are shown a row of women carrying their babies on their backs; their tall head-gear probably denotes a mode of hairdressing worn by married women. The panel below this shows three men with beards and hats. The figures of this group are depicted with considerable differences of individual character, both in costumes and attitudes as well as personal characteristics shown in each head; possibly they are intended to depict particular chiefs or other persons of importance in the State; they appear to have no special occupation, except that the central figure carries an object attached to his elbow, perhaps a basket.

The lowest panel shows a native official or perhaps merchant driving before him two slaves, a man and a woman. The man is dressed in a pair of black trousers only, and the woman wears only a black waist-band; their arms are bound at the elbows behind their backs. The hairdressing of the woman is like that of the married women above.

In the large panel on the right is shown the white man, dressed in a yellow suit and pith helmet and with a small black moustache. He is carried in a hammock or litter, in which he sits bolt upright looking upwards with haughty mien. This mode of conveyance is said to be used for persons of rank, though its introduction into Africa is comparatively recent; it is said to have been brought by the Portuguese from Brazil, where its use was confined to the purpose of sleeping.

The panel above shows a man on horseback holding reins and followed by two attendants carrying baggage; it is perhaps intended to depict the white man's assistant, preceding him. The lower panel shows a group of men marching in line and carrying staves. The one below that shows a group of baggage-carriers marching abreast with boxes on their heads, and bags in their hands, one bag between two persons. The background of this panel is plain and coloured red, whereas those of the other panels are variously coloured and carved with patterns. The lowest panel, mostly painted black, shows a group of four men; these figures are much damaged, but possibly depict soldiers, judging by their uniform hats and waist-belts; in every case their arms are broken off.

These relief carvings bear comparison in some respects with ancient Semitic and Egyptian bas-reliefs, in the manner of visualizing a very comprehensive subject and creating, by the use of design and variations in relative proportions, all sorts of varied scenes not naturally visible together; the rows of figures paraded in line also can compare with parallel Semitic work. The great depth of relief, however, enables the Yoruba carver to represent positions for the figures, outside the scope of Semitic sculpture, by means of showing them from a three-quarter view.

PLATE XII

A CHIEF WITH HIS WIVES

Figure group representing a seated chief with his wives, children, attendants, and live stock, probably engaged in an ancestral religious ceremony.

Earthenware; H. 20″; Diam. (base) 14″.
No recorded provenance.
Probably Fanti tribe, Gold Coast Colony.
British Museum.

This group is modelled in one piece, except for some minor details which are separate. The pottery is unburnished, the colour being red ochre (burnt sienna). The base (5½″ high) is circular and hollow; its surface is covered with an impressed pattern made while the clay was soft; the instrument used may have been the corn-cob, divested of its grains.[1]

The specimen is one of a collection of three, of which no records have been preserved, except that they are placed in the 'Nigeria' case in the British Museum; they were probably early acquisitions, not later than last century. The only other example of this style of work known to the writer is one—smaller and partly broken —in the Liverpool Museum—of which the label reads: 'from the Fantee, Gold Coast'; the old-fashioned spelling of this name suggests that the label is an old and authentic ascription, and not a recent surmise.

That this group is Fanti work, and represents a family of that tribe, is further supported by descriptions of these peace-loving kinsmen of the war-like Ashanti. Unlike the latter with their large centralized community, the Fanti are, according to the *Living Races of Mankind*,[2] 'a tribe of village communities; they live in small villages, presided over by the head of the family as chief.'

Another description, which might almost be taken for the subject of this group, has been given by T. E. Bowdich[3] who stopped a short while at the Fanti village of Chief Payntree, during his mission to Ashanti in 1817; 'I walked with Mr. Tedlie along a very neat path, well fenced, and divided by stiles, to a corn plantation of at least twenty acres, and well cultivated. Payntree's farm-house was situated here, and afforded superior conveniences: a fowl-house, a pigeon-house, and a large granary raised on a strong stage. . . . The order, cleanliness, and comfort surprised us; the sun had just set, and a cheerful fire on a clean hearth supported the evening meal. The old man was seated in his state chair, diverting himself with his children

[1] R. S. Rattray, *Religion and Art in Ashanti*, pp. 302, 303.

[2] Hutchinson, p. 363.
[3] *Mission to Ashantee*, London, 1873, p. 17.

and younger wives; the elder one was looking on from the opposite apartment with happy indifference; it was the first scene of domestic comfort I had witnessed among the natives.'

The family or community, depicted in this group, appear to be engaged in a religious ceremony, with a priest summoning the god with the beating of his gong, while an animal sacrifice is made before the shrine of the god (?) and the chest of the ancestors (?).

Apart from its subject, the group is probably itself an implement of worship, for use as a temporary residence for ancestors; thus it has the element of the unbroken chain, in so far as it depicts ancestors engaged in ancestral worship!

The figure seated in the centre of the group depicts presumably the chief or head of the family, his rank being indicated by the fan and the staff held in each hand, and also by his hat, which is detachable, and resembles the nineteenth-century European style of 'top-hat'. The two female figures seated on either side are either his wives or female relatives of rank. Their long robes and elaborate mode of hairdressing correspond to styles said to be specially characteristic of Fanti women, whose dress consists 'of a brightly coloured loin-cloth, which among married women is increased to a wrap that covers from the breast to the ankles',[1] and whose hair 'is worked into a knob-shaped chignon, a pair of horn-shaped projections'.[1] One of the two women suckles a baby which lies across her knees. The other woman holds a naked boy in front of her; she is also pregnant, and wears three charms on a necklace suspended between the breasts; these are probably amulets such as are worn during pregnancy as a protection against witchcraft or evil influences.[2]

The three smaller figures in front are either attendants or priests; each of them wears a cap covered with tufts. One of them is engaged in beating a gong, probably the *odawuru*, iron gong, 'used in religious ceremonies for summoning the spirit of a god.'[3] Another of them has both hands holding a sacrificial domestic animal, which is tethered and is probably a ram, judging by its small horns and large drooping ears, an animal commonly used in religious sacrifices, particularly of ancestor worship. This figure also wears, suspended from the right shoulder, a string of bells or rattles, probably the 'fetish charms' or *suman*,[4] such as are carried by priests. The figure in the centre has both hands holding a two-legged table on which is placed a circular basin with a flat lid, which is detached. This is probably

[1] *Living Races of Mankind*, p. 363.
[2] R. S. Rattray, *Religion and Art in Ashanti*, pp. 54, 67.
[3] R. S. Rattray, *Ashanti*, p. 174; also cf.

a similar figure on a brass vessel, *kuduo*, in possession of Lord Baden-Powell (*Religion and Art in Ashanti*, Fig. 54).
[4] R. S. Rattray, *Ashanti*, p. 90.

intended to represent the shrine of a god. Comparison with one of the companion specimens in the British Museum shows a similar object supported on the head of one of the figures; this is said to be the customary manner of carrying a brass pan or basin when used as a shrine. Among the Ashanti, whose customs are largely similar to those of the Fanti, the pan is said to contain 'various ingredients', and 'upon certain definite occasions, becomes the temporary dwelling, or resting-place, of a non-human spirit or spirits.'[1]

In the forefront of the group is a rectangular box with a detached lid, the top of which is ornamented with incised patterns; this object may be intended for an ancestral chest like the brass coffers,[2] formerly in the sacred Mausoleum of the Ashanti Kings at Bantama previous to its being set on fire by the British Expedition of 1895.

The details depicted in this group appear to be such as belong to the higher aspects of the Twi religion, illustrative of which may be appended a song taken down by Rattray[3] from a priest, who, heavily adorned with *suman*, was beating his gong while he sang:

> My words reach far away, O Ame Yao.
> My words reach peoples.
> I who am the Son of the God Ta Kese,
> King of Abau
> My words reach peoples.
> Father, help me for I am miserable.
> Father Ta Kese, help me for I am unhappy.
> Ati Akosua, help me for I am unhappy.

PLATE XIII
THREE-FACED MASK

Skin-covered head with three faces and surmounted by artificial horns.

Wood; H. 13⅝".
Stated to be 'from Cameroons'.
Probably Ekoi tribe, Cross River.
Horniman Museum.

This mask is intended for wearing on the top of the head at dances.[4] The skin is brown-orange in colour, darkened by age, and is decorated with black paint, making a thin stain like dark chocolate. An unusual peculiarity is its combination of three faces; two of these are light coloured with hair, eyebrows, and facial marks stained dark; while the third face (showing to the left in the photograph) has the effect

[1] R. S. Rattray, *Ashanti*, p. 145.
[2] Op. cit., p. 120, and p. 117, quoting Baden-Powell, *The Downfall of Prempeh.*
[3] *Ashanti*, pp. 201, 202.
[4] See notes to masks of the same type, Plate XVII.

reversed, being dark coloured with the features light. The two former have no disks shown on the temples as on the latter. The eyes are metal and the teeth pieces of cane; the basket-base is entirely covered by the skin.

PLATE XIV

APRONED WOMAN; MAN IN CAP; MAN WITH DRESSED HAIR

Figure of a woman, probably representing a twin, with an apron of coral beads (left in photograph).

Hard wood; H. 26½"; W. 3¾"; D. 4".

Mendi tribe, Sierra Leone.

Horniman Museum.

This figure is one of a pair representing a man[1] and a woman; it is thinly painted black, which, on the light-coloured wood, shows dull grey. The arms are rendered alike, with hands placed either side of the navel; the legs and feet are slightly separated. The hair in the form of a double crest with vertical grooves on the sides, depicts a type of hairdressing worn by women of the Upper Mendi tribe,[2] except as regards the rosettes on each side, which may be intended for the bunches of seeds which are worn in the hair by Mendi girls after initiation into the Bundu Society.[2]

On the front and back of the body are designs consisting of incised lines within a rectangular space. These probably depict the very fine cicatrization of the skin worn in a similar manner by Mendi women.[2] The figure also has two horn-like ornaments on the throat; these are absent in the companion male figure. They appear to represent the leopard's teeth worn in this manner by Mendi women; but A. R. Wright[3] describes them as 'horns having a fetish meaning'.

The usual type of small female figure, made by the Mendi, is called *minsereh* and used for divination.[4] The fact that this figure has a male companion suggests that it is not one of these, but that the pair represent twins. Such figures are said to be made as portraits of actual twin children; when one of them dies, the survivor receives the image of his deceased companion.[5]

Figure of a man wearing a cap (centre in photograph).

Hard wood; H. 28"; Diam. (base) 6½".

No recorded provenance.

Probably region of the Ogowai River, Gabun.

Wellcome Historical Medical Museum.

[1] Not included in the plate.
[2] T. J. Alldridge, *The Sherbro and its Hinterland*, Figs. 34, 44.
[3] *Folk-Lore*, vol. xviii, p. 424.
[4] Alldridge, op. cit., pp. 145, 147.
[5] H. U. Hall, *The Museum Journal,* Philadelphia, Dec. 1928, p. 414.

H

The figure is carved in dark-coloured wood and is entirely painted brownish-black. The bead decoration consists of a wire necklace threaded with a single grey stone, and wrist-bands of glass trade beads, those on the right wrist being red, except one string which is green.

The figure is covered on body, arms, and head with designs carved in relief, a process necessitating the chiselling away of the entire rest of the surface. These depict cicatrizations of the skin, somewhat like those worn by the Apingi of the Ogowai River, according to sketches and descriptions given by Du Chaillu.[1]

The decoration of the back of the head is probably intended for a cap made of beads, perhaps like the one made of white beads which Du Chaillu[2] saw worn by the Queen of the Fans and generally admired, at his reception among them.

The base on which the figure stands is hollow. It closely resembles the wooden footstools[3] carved by the Fan, and is probably intended for one of those utensils.

Despite these indications of the Fan workmanship, to which must be added a similarity to their usual figure carving, in the pose of the head on the long upright neck, it is unlikely that the figure is actually a work of theirs; this conclusion is chiefly based on the form of cicatrices, and on the treatment of the eyes, which in Fan carvings are nearly always of metal or pottery and inlaid.

There is, however, every reason to suppose that it is a work of a neighbouring tribe—though not possible to assign a name—in contact with the Fan, whose carvings are among the masterpieces of West African art.

Figure of a man with dressed hair (right in photograph).

> Hard wood; H. 25"; W. 5¼"; D. 5".
> No recorded provenance.
> Probably region of the Ogowai River, Gabun.
> *Wellcome Historical Medical Museum.*

In colour and material the figure resembles the preceding one, and has a necklace threaded with a single large nut. It also has anklets, the one round the left ankle consisting of black and white cut stones. The other strings of glass trade beads have probably been substituted when the older strings got broken.

The designs on the face, depicting cicatrices, are very similar to those of the preceding figure, but those on the body are less elaborate.

The decoration of the head is probably a representation of a mode of hairdressing somewhat like the pig-tails worn by the Fan.

[1] *Adventures in Equatorial Africa*, London, 1861, p. 442.
[2] Op. cit., p. 77.
[3] Günter Tessmann, *Die Pangwe*, Berlin, 1913, vol. i, Fig. 40.

PLATE XV
WOMAN'S HEAD

Mask probably representing a woman's head.

Soft wood; H. 11¾"; W. 7½"; D. 4".
Stated to be 'from Lahou, Ivory Coast'.
Probably Baoule or Guerret tribes.
Bristol Museum, 1914.

The wood is light in colour but is thinly painted black. The mask is part of the same collection as the figure and mat shown in Plate VI. It depicts a person's head with skin cicatrices in front of each ear, resembling the row of small neat scars worn in this manner by Ivory Coast tribes, notably the Guerret.[1]

The hair is represented in a manner almost invariably shown in Ivory Coast carvings, and represents a style prevalent among the tribes of that region. Judging by photographs[1] of Guerret men and women, it is obtained by parting the hair each side; the two side portions are brushed downwards, while the central mass is gathered into a crest with the ends neatly knotted down its centre; all the edges are carefully sewn with a fine border. In some cases there are also small bunches of hair twisted into narrow-pointed projections somewhat resembling a ram's horns. It is these latter which are probably depicted by the two projections shown on each side of the mask, which in other examples are often extended to represent long-curved horns.

As this style of hair-dressing is worn alike by men and women, it is not possible to determine to which sex the mask belongs, but the absence of beard indicates that it probably represents a woman.

It is intended to be worn covering only the face and is probably employed in religious dances.

PLATE XVI
WOMEN ANCESTORS' MASKS

Mask representing the head of a woman (right in photograph).

Soft wood; painted; L. 16½"; H. 9"; W. 7½".
Stated to be 'from the Interior of Lagos, West Africa'.
Probably Egba (Yoruba) tribe, W. Nigeria.
Brighton Public Museum, before 1890. (James Ashbury Collection.)

[1] Cf. photographic series G. Lerat, Exposition Coloniale, Paris, 1931.

51

Another similar mask (left in photograph).

    Soft wood; painted; L. $16\frac{1}{2}''$; H. $9\frac{1}{4}''$; W. $7\frac{1}{4}''$.

    Probably Egba (Yoruba) tribe, W. Nigeria.

    Brighton Public Museum, before 1890. (James Ashbury Collection.)

In both masks the wood is light-coloured, but with the outside surface entirely covered with paint. The colours are: face, dark purplish-brown; eyes, white; eye-lashes and facial marks, dark blue (prussian); hair, black; forehead band, same colour as face but with the addition of a pattern in blue, black, and white. The masks are hollow inside, but are intended to cover only the person's face; there are small apertures consisting of a very narrow slit between the lips, and two holes in the nostrils (about $\frac{1}{2}''$ diam.). There are also holes in the eyes to represent the pupils; but these are bored only to a depth of $\frac{3}{4}''$. The upper part of each mask depicts a form of hairdressing worn by married women,[1] thus indicating that the masks are intended to represent persons of that sex; and the triple marks on each cheek represent the gashes worn as tribal marks by the Egba.[1]

    The two masks are very similar to one another as regards both measurements and details, and are probably intended as a pair; but they differ in facial type; for example, the one on the left has forehead longer but nose shorter than the one on the right, and chin protruding more, making a less vertical angle from forehead to chin.

    The masks belong to a distinct type of which various versions are commonly found in collections,[2] owing to the early trade and missionary settlements at Lagos, whence they were obtained.

    Masks are worn among the Yoruba in connexion with rites or dances of secret societies, chiefly those of *Egungun* and of *Oro*; the dances of the former society take place on occasions of a person's death; and according to P. A. Talbot,[3] the masks which are worn by the participants probably represent 'the ancestors who had returned to life for the occasion'. In these dances 'the Images, dressed in their long robes with a net or wooden mask over the face, parade the streets, jumping about, uttering sentences in an artificial voice and accompanied by friends who keep the bystanders at a distance with their long wands. . . . In several ways it resembles the European Christmas, as it is an occasion for the reunion of the family and of friends and is treated as a general holiday.'

    Possibly these two masks were carved together as a pair, and were intended to portray two female ancestors who were twins. The masks are apparently old ones;

[1] Cf. Pl. IV.

[2] Cf. particularly fine examples in the Museums of Edinburgh, Liverpool, Halifax, Horniman, and Wellcome Historical Medical Museum.

[3] *Southern Nigeria*, vol. iii.

their clearly defined and precise form of carving with the aspect of an intellectual and cultural type, indicates that they date from before the era of modern European influence. The style resembles that of Benin work but has probably evolved from an older Yoruba tradition, from which the Benin style similarly grew.

PLATE XVII

CRESTED HEAD AND TWO-FACED HORNED HEAD

Skin-covered head with two faces and four artificial horns (right in photograph).

Soft wood; H. $13\frac{1}{2}$"; W. (horns) $9\frac{1}{4}$"; D. (horns) $10\frac{1}{2}$".
No recorded provenance.
Probably Ekoi tribe, Cross River, Southern Nigeria.
Wellcome Historical Medical Museum.

The mask is carved in wood and covered with skin, except the horns, eyes, and mouth; the colour of the skin, which is probably that of a human being, is bright lemon-yellow but darkened by age, and parts of it (showing dark in the photograph) are thinly painted black. The eyes are formed by pieces of metal with black pegs of hard wood for the pupils; the teeth consist of thin pieces of cane inserted in the upper lip. The circular disks on the temples and bridge of the nose are raised in low relief; those on the temples of the rear face, however, consist of three disks in a row, one above the other, instead of a single one. In a fine old mask of the same type, in the Liverpool Museum, these marks are shown as lumps resembling keloids. Probably they are tribal marks, like those worn by the Ibo, Ekoi, and Efik tribes, and formed, according to Talbot,[1] by 'a mixture of ground charcoal and palm oil', rubbed into the skin and 'renewed about every six months'; Dr. Baikie[2] describes them as 'round spots each about the size of a pea'. The row of three spots appears to be the race mark of the Ekoi, from whom it must have been borrowed by the Efik, who in Dr. Baikie's time had recently adopted it. The single spot, on the other hand, is probably the Ibo mark,[3] borrowed by both the other tribes. The intermingling of these tribal marks adds to the difficulty of ascertaining the provenance of the mask as between either of the three tribes mentioned above.

The other designs on the face resemble an Ekoi mode of decoration of which the black dye, according to Talbot,[4] is made from a flower like a wild hyacinth.

According to the same author, masks of this type are 'used at war dances',[5] as

[1] *In the Shadow of the Bush,* p. 319.
[2] *Narrative of an Exploring Voyage,* London, 1856, p. 351.
[3] Cf. Pl. XX.
[4] Op. cit., p. 319.
[5] *Southern Nigeria,* vol. iii, Fig. 189.

substitutes for the freshly killed heads of enemies which formerly were borne by the victors.[1] The skin used for the mask is probably therefore taken from a captured enemy; the tribal marks being either the victim's, or the captor's superimposed.

The dances are probably those of the Egbo Secret Society,[2] one of whose members, concealed by a costume, wears the mask resting on the top of his head, with cloth draped round its base. Though it might appear that its use is that of a gruesome relic brandished by exulting victors, this is far from the case; its use is of religious significance connected with the supreme deity, whom it either represents or is supposed to be transformed into. The two faces are said by Talbot[2] to be 'one male and the other female', representing 'the omniscience of the Deity looking both ways, into the future and back to the past, as also the bi-sexual character shown in the oldest conceptions of Obassi Osaw and Onassi Nsi, sky-father and earth mother'.

This characteristic and the association with war inevitably recall the two-faced Roman divinity, Janus, from whom, in view of the ancient history of this region, in so far as it is known, it may be actually derived.

The type appears to be widely distributed over the region of the Cross River, which accounts for ascriptions given, in other examples, both to the Cameroons and different parts of Nigeria. Two very old examples, of which the provenance is established, are those brought back by Governor Beecroft from his expedition up the Cross River in 1843;[3] and this mask is undoubtedly from the same region.

Skin-covered head with a tall crest.

> Soft wood; H. 18"; W. 5"; D. 7¼".
> No provenance recorded.
> Probably Ekoi tribe, S. Nigeria.
> *British Museum*, 1911. (Collected by E. Dayrell, District Commissioner, Ikorn District, S. Nigeria.)

This mask, unlike the preceding one, consists of a single face only; it is intended for wearing on the top of the head at dances, in the manner described above.

The skin is bright yellow-orange in colour, and is decorated with black paint; the skin, however, does not cover the tall crest. The latter includes a pair of spirals at the front, probably a variation of the more frequently shown wooden imitations of antelope horns (an example of which is shown by its shadow cast on the background[4]). The four small disks painted on each side of the neck are perhaps

---

[1] *In the Shadow of the Bush*, p. 261.
[2] Op. cit., p. 44.
[3] In Bankfield Museum, Halifax.

[4] Skin-covered head surmounted by a tall spiral horn made of wood (Wellcome Historical Medical Museum).

derived from the tribal marks usually placed on each temple, but now being no longer worn, are depicted in a purely formal manner; there is also a design painted down the back of the neck. The eyes and teeth are like those in the adjoining mask, but show more clearly the two partially filed front teeth, representing an Ekoi custom, now dying out.[1]

PLATE XVIII

BOY'S INITIATION MASK WITH PLAITED HAIR

Mask with long plaits of fibre.

> Wood; H. 11″; W. 7″; D. 12″.
> Stated to be 'from Ba-Pende tribe'.
> Probably between Dumba and Kangala, Loange River, Belgian Congo.
> *British Museum*, 1910. (Collected by E. Torday, 1909.)

The natural colour of the wood is light, but, with the exception of the teeth, it has been thinly painted dark reddish-brown resembling mahogany in colour, and white for lips, ears, and a double row of spots over the forehead. The former colour is probably intended to represent the Ba-Pende custom of colouring themselves with 'the red *takula* dye'.[2]

There is a small circular projection, carved in front of each ear, which depicts, the skin cicatrice worn as a tribal mark by the Ba-Pende.[3] The top and back of the mask consists of a thick pad of cloth, woven from raphia-palm, dyed black, and covered with fibre-ends—partially worn away; and attached to it are four long coils also of plaited fibre, dyed black. This represents the Ba-Pende mode of hairdressing, in which the hair is formed into 'little tassels resembling a mop on the top' of the head, and, if not naturally long enough, is replaced by a wig.[4] The piece of woven raphia cloth hanging down at the back is of raw sienna colour and is intended for covering the wearer's neck; the apertures to enable him to see and breathe consist only of slits in the eyes and holes in the nostrils.

The mask was collected by the late Emil Torday, probably in one of the Ba-Pende villages which he passed through between the Lubue and Loange Rivers. The purpose of the mask is said to be for wearing during initiation ceremonies by candidates for circumcision. The costume with which it was worn is of plain brown grass cloth with long sleeves, judging by a photograph[5] which shows the mask worn

---

[1] P. A. Talbot, *In the Shadow of the Bush*, p. 319.
[2] M. W. Hilton-Simpson, *Land and Peoples of the Kasai*, p. 280.
[3] E. Torday and T. A. Joyce, *Les Bushongo*, pp. 166, 167.
[4] *Land and Peoples of the Kasai*, p. 280.
[5] E. Torday, *Causeries Congolaises*, Fig. 38.

by a Ba-Pende boy. 'During this ceremony, which lasts several days, the lads have to spend all their time in the forest or in the bush, and are obliged to keep out of sight of other people';[1] and it is firmly believed 'that if a woman sets eyes on one of these masks she will die'.

The masks carved for the purpose described above form a distinct type. Though this mask is an example of the type, it is far from typical, chiefly on account of its long straight nose without the usual sharply pointed tilt upwards. The pointed nose, characteristic of Ba-Pende art, has clearly been borrowed from the wood-carving style of their south-western neighbours, the Ba-Yaka, an influence which appears to be entirely and unusually absent in the carving of this mask, the work, perhaps, of an 'individualist' carver.

PLATE XIX

GHOST MASK OF A WOMAN

Mask of a woman's head with painted face, red and white, probably a ghost.

Soft wood; painted; H. 11"; W. 7"; D. 6".

Stated to be 'from Sette Cama'.

Probably Ashira or Ashango tribes, Gabun.

British Museum, 1904. (Hon. W. Rothschild Collection.)

The mask is hollow and intended for wearing over the face, with narrow apertures in the eyes to see through. The wood is light-coloured, but the face and hair are painted, the face being white, except for the forehead and lips, which are bright red (vermilion), and the hair being black. Probably the unpainted portion below the chin and surrounding the back of the head was intended to be covered by the costume of the wearer.

This mask belongs to a distinct type, unmistakable by its semi-closed eyes of crescent shape, its elaborate coiffure, and its aspect resembling—by some unaccountable coincidence—works of Japanese or Chinese sculpture, and is fit to rank among masterpieces of West African art.

Examples of this type, of which there are only a few in public collections,[2] are accompanied by scarcely more information regarding provenance or function than is the case with this mask. Its provenance, 'Sette Cama', indicates only that it was purchased—probably by a passing trader—at the coastal town of that name, whither it must previously have been brought from the interior, possibly with some slave caravan of the past.

[1] M. W. Hilton-Simpson, op. cit., p. 280.
[2] Cf. two examples in Liverpool Museum (one illustrated by L. Frobenius, *Die* *Masken*, 1898, Fig. 53), examples at Oxford, Pitt-Rivers Museum (ibid., Fig. 52), and Manchester University Museum.

This type of mask divides into two kinds, which differ mainly in having either the face depicted with skin cicatrices or being without as in this case. Two examples of the latter kind, in the Museums of Oxford and Manchester, are described respectively 'Ivili' and 'Akira': the former is the name of a tribe, kinsmen of the Bavili, who are only likely to have obtained the mask from a neighbour; the latter, however, may be another spelling of 'Ashira', the name of a tribe which may very well be the provenance of this mask.

The Ashira, like several of the tribes dwelling on the Ogowai River, including their rather remote kinsmen the Ashango, dress their hair in an elaborate style[1] which that of this mask is clearly intended to represent, namely a bunch on the top of the head, built over a framework of old pieces of grass-cloth, sometimes embellished with similar bunches on each side, the hair around these erections being carefully shaved up to the edge.

Furthermore the Ashira, unlike some of their neighbours,[2] with the exception of the Ashango, are reported to wear no facial cicatrices: in this respect also the mask bears out a resemblance.

A particular feature of its face is the very thin eyebrow lines; it is difficult to determine whether these are intended as such, or as if shaved off. The point is one which would help to solve its provenance as between Ashira and Ashango, for the former leave their eyebrows alone, but the latter remove them and pluck out their eyelashes.[3]

The combination of red and white colours shown on the mask is commonly used among both Ashira and Ashango,[4] and probably among some of their neighbours, for decorating the face and also for painting religious figures. The red colour is said to be a powder called *ntchingo,*[5] 'made by rubbing two pieces of barwood together', which is afterwards boiled and mixed with clay.

A peculiarity in the mask is the intense brilliance of the red, which gives an unusual luminosity and accentuates its ghostlike aspect. Its function was undoubtedly for wearing in dances, and probably by some one impersonating a spirit or ghost.[6] That the subject was a female is indicated by the hairdressing being that of a woman. In the Ogowai region, the chief women's secret society is that called *Njembe,*[7] and the mask may have belonged originally to a leader of this society.

[1] P. Du Chaillu, *A Journey to Ashango-land,* London, 1867, pp. 286, 331; and *Adventures in Equatorial Africa,* 1861, p. 416.

[2] *A Journey to Ashango-land,* p. 255.

[3] Op. cit., p. 331.

[4] Op. cit., p. 286; and *Adventures in Equatorial Africa,* p. 410.

[5] *A Journey to Ashango-land,* pp. 286, 331.

[6] H. U. Hall, *The Museum Journal,* December 1927.

[7] *Adventures in Equatorial Africa,* p. 294.

I

DESCRIPTION OF PLATES

WHITE MASK WITH SCARLET EYES

Mask representing a person's head wearing combs and ornamental hairdressing.

Hard wood; painted; H. 12″; W. 7″; D. 11″.
Stated to be 'from Ogenegbode (Agenibode), S. Nigeria'.
Probably Ibo tribe.
Cambridge University Museum.

The mask is carved from a single piece of light-coloured wood, except the eyes which consist of a circle of brilliant scarlet seeds (*Abrus precatorius*)—now mostly missing—set in a black glutinous substance. The rest of the mask has been painted; the face being white (now mostly worn away), the eyebrows and hair black with white in the crevices, and the facial marks blue (ultramarine), with traces of the same colour on cheeks and ears. In its present condition the mask is not complete, a crest along the centre of the head having been broken off (showing in Plate XXI as a light band). Comparisons with other examples of the same type[1] show that the missing piece must have been a very tall crest or head-dress 8″ long by 1″ thick and about 5″ high, repeating in shape the curve of the crown, and ornamented with white disks (similar to those bordering its base) and possibly surmounted by a row of small tufts. It may have been broken off while still in native use; for the back of the head, which is also broken, has been carefully mended by rejoining two loose pieces with cane riveting.

The mask belongs to a distinct type, but comparison[1] with other examples does not help in the elucidation of its provenance or use by the provision of actual records. That it is, however, a work of the Ibo tribe is proved by the close resemblance of its hair to that worn by Ibo women of Awka, Onitsha Province, judging by two photographs reproduced by Northcote Thomas.[2] These show the hair decorated with coils as on this mask, obtained by being 'allowed to grow to considerable length and then twisted and plaited tightly so that coils are formed all over the head and then, fastened with skilful manipulation to the short hair'. They also show the tall crest on the centre of the head with a row of small tufts (represented by the part now

---

[1] Cf. examples in the museums of the University of Manchester and of Oxford (two specimens), Batley, Liverpool, Halifax, and Philadelphia, U.S.A. (reproduced in the *Museum Journal*, March 1920) and New York, American Museum of Natural History (reproduced in the *Journal*, by Clark Wissler, July 1928 but described, presumably incorrectly, as 'mask from New Ireland'); cf. also *In the Shadow of the Bush*, Plate, p. 58.

[2] *People of All Nations*, ed. J. A. Hammerton, pp. 527, 563.

missing in the mask), which is said to be a 'crest of wood ornamented with large pearl buttons' and 'tightly secured on the top of her head'. This description indicates that the row of white disks on the crown of the mask are intended for pearl buttons.

The face of the mask has various patterns carved in relief, including a small rosette in front of each ear. The latter is probably intended for the Ibo tribal mark or skin cicatrice, as indicated by Dr. Baikie.[1] Comparison with other examples of this type of mask show the same tribal marks, triple[2] or single, as on the skin-covered type. Presumably both types have a somewhat similar provenance, probably that part of the Ibo territory adjoining the Ekoi and the Efik.

The mask has a row of small holes along its base; these are presumably for attaching a costume to cover face and neck.[3]

The function of the mask is undoubtedly for wearing at religious dances or ceremonies, probably by men despite its feminine coiffure, judging by the words of a label attached, reading, 'Male Mask (*Aule*)'; these dances are probably in connexion with the propitiation of ghosts and hostile spirits. The latter surmise is indicated by the scarlet seeds in the eyes, which in some parts of Nigeria are associated with death;[4] their brilliant hue serves to emphasize the surrounding whiteness of the face, and gives it a lurid aspect. The white paint also indicates the same function, being used to denote hostile spirits; the latter notion has resulted in white travellers experiencing an hostility in the form of a 'colour bar', peculiarly comparable to that suffered by coloured persons in 'white' countries; for example Mungo Park,[5] when exhibited in 1797 to the wives of the King of Ludamar, caused them to shudder with disgust, while his nankeen breeches which resembled the colour of his skin and closely fitted his body were considered not only unseemly but indecent.

PLATE XXII
WATER POT WITH A FRIEZE IN RELIEF

Water vessel ornamented with human heads and figures of snakes eating frogs.

Black earthenware; H. 9½"; Diam. 12".

Stated to be 'from Ashanti, Gold Coast'.

British Museum, 1917. (Collected by F. M. Viscount Wolseley.)

This vessel was probably acquired by Lord Wolseley while he was on the Gold Coast in connexion with the first Ashanti War in 1873–4, and was probably an old specimen when collected.

[1] See notes, Pl. XVII.
[2] Cf. example in Manchester Museum with a row of three marks on each temple.
[3] Cf. example with woollen garment and padded neck-covering in Batley Museum.
[4] Cf. mask, Bauchi tribe (British Museum).
[5] *Travels in the Interior of Africa*, Everyman ed., p. 101.

59

It is made of thick earthenware with black, shiny, and burnished surface. In shape it belongs to the type called *ahena*, large pot used for carrying water.[1] The black glaze is obtained by a process of 'smoking', by means of quenching the fire with water so that it emits a dense smoke which permeates the heated clay with 'a mixture of finely divided tar and carbon'.[1]

The ornament is in the form of a frieze, and consists, twice repeated, of the representation of a human face—or the mask of one—and the figure of a snake eating a frog.

Though the form of the vessel is typically Ashanti, the frieze is not so, either in subject or treatment. The subject is one commonly represented in Benin art, either in the form of a snake devouring a frog,[2] or devouring a human head,[2] or in the combination of all three.[3]

In modelling, however, the vessel does not resemble the Benin specimens, which are detailed in pattern, and in which the frog, for example, is short-legged and squat.

The same subject also appears elsewhere, namely carved on some paddles[4] which are undoubtedly from the Ivory Coast region (Kong tribe?).

These coincidences can only be accounted for by the subject, having been copied by one people from the other. Possibly the original was a Benin work—perhaps a royal stool sent as a present; a copy may have been made in the Ivory Coast and thence recopied by the Ashanti, or more probably modelled by the latter under the influence of their highly artistic neighbours—perhaps in fact by a Kong artist at work in the Ashanti Kingdom.

PLATE XXIII
LIDDED VESSEL FOR CEREMONIAL USE

Vessel and lid, covered with figures modelled in relief.

Earthenware; painted; H. 12″; L. 12½″; W. 11¾″.
Stated to be 'from Dahomey'.
Probably from Abomey, capital of Dahomey.
Halifax, Bankfield Museum, formerly in Whitby Museum. (Governor Beecroft Collection, probably 1850.)

This vessel was collected by Governor John Beecroft while he was in West Africa

[1] R. S. Rattray, *Religion and Art in Ashanti*, p. 304, Fig. 242.
[2] See specimens in the British Museum, and H. Ling Roth, *Great Benin*, p. 90.
[3] H. Ling Roth, op. cit., Fig. 111 (two royal stools in possession of Sir Ralph Moor). Also von Sydow, *Die Kunst der Naturvölker*, p. 97 (apparently same specimen as above, now in Berlin Museum).
[4] Collection of Curtis Moffat, Esq.

between 1840 and 1854, and was probably obtained by him during one of the two visits he made to the Dahomey King Gezo at Abomey, in 1850 and 1852, while he was British Consul for the Bight of Biafra. The vessel is therefore an old one.

The colour of the background part of the vessel is red ochre; the other colours are white (varying from that of cream to greenish-blue) and very dark brown (varying from that of chocolate to deep crimson); the vessel is broken in places and considerably chipped. The lid is separate, and has a small handle at the apex; and the base rests on four small circular feet.

The frieze of figures and other ornaments are moulded in the earthenware in high relief and interspersed with impressed patterns; they include figures in which the feet are shown in front view, unlike in bas-reliefs of the ancient Mediterranean peoples, wherein human feet are usually represented sideways.

The style of work is based on the painted wood carving of the Lagos (Yoruba) 'school',[1] judging by its subjects, attitudes, and costumes. No other example, however, of similar bas-relief modelling is known to the author except a small fragment in the British Museum. The latter is stated to be from 'Southern Nigeria'. Nevertheless this vessel is undoubtedly Dahomey work, as stated on its label, and, moreover, is probably from Abomey, capital of Dahomey, judging by photographs and drawings[2] of the mural decorations of the Royal Palace and temples at Abomey, which are described as 'Bas-reliefs en terre sur les murs' and include rosettes and other stamped curvilinear designs somewhat resembling those on this vessel.

The original label attached to the vessel describes it as a 'Fetish object'. This description, though vague in meaning, indicates that it had a sacred or ceremonial use, probably in accordance with the information given by P. Bouche,[3] that it was the custom in Dahomey 'to place beside certain fetishes vases having lids of clay and in them offerings intended for the fetishes'.

The decorative arrangement of the vessel appears to be divided into two parts, a frieze round the lower part depicting officials or servants of the State, and that of the lid depicting divinities and religious emblems. Thus the lower part may be meant to represent the living material world, and the upper part the supernatural or divine.

The details on the lower part of the vessel appear to be as follows: On the side (right in photograph), a naked prisoner (dark brown) holds in his left hand a bag (?) in front of his body, and stretches his right hand across his chest so as to

---

[1] Cf. Pl. I.
[2] A. le Herissé, *L'Ancien Royaume de Dahomey*, Paris, 1911, Pl. iv; E. G. Waterlot, *Les Bas-reliefs des bâtiments royaux d'Abomey*, Paris, 1926.

[3] *La Côte des Esclaves et le Dahomey*, p. 396 (quoted by H. U. Hall, *The Museum Journal*, Philadelphia, September 1924, p. 198).

rest it on his left shoulder; he has a white halter round his neck, the other end of which is held by a chief (white) wearing a flat circular cap; the latter figure is riding on horse-back with saddle and stirrups, holding the reins (deep crimson) in his right hand; he is preceded by a soldier (dark brown) wearing a cap and trousers striped, like the costumes of most of the figures; he holds a circular shield (greenish-blue) and a sword. On the end (left in photograph), a figure of a woman (dark brown) with an elaborate coiffure and wearing a skirt, holds in her left hand an unidentified ceremonial object; at her side is the figure of a man wearing cap and trousers and holding objects resembling rattles in each hand. On the rear side (not shown in photograph) there are three figures, namely a man holding weapons, a man (white) holding a sceptre (?), and a girl holding with both hands a bowl in front of her, probably intended as a religious offering. On the rear end (not shown in photograph) there are two figures and two animals, namely a man playing a flute,[1] and another (dark brown) holding a spear and also a cord tied round the neck of a cow, which bears a chameleon of similar size on its back.

The details on the lid are as follows: On the side (right in photograph) a figure of a nude woman (white) suckles a child (dark brown); her left arm is bent, so that her head lies on her hand; with her right hand she draws towards her the head of the child whose hands and feet are in positions of clinging to its mother; her hair is grooved in the style of Yoruba married women; possibly this figure may represent the mother-goddess, Odudua.[2] Behind her back is the figure of a lizard, a creature connected with religious practices.[3] Seen in this position it recalls the Ashanti proverb[4] which runs: 'It is difficult to throw a stone at a lizard which is clinging to a pot (without breaking the pot).' At the far end is a river fish (mud or shad), a subject frequent in both Yoruba and Ashanti work; below are two tadpoles, a horn, and a chain for obtaining good luck[5] (?); the trumpet-shaped object beyond the figure is probably a religious implement called by le Herissé[6] 'Asën, ou objet de culte', and said to be stuck into the earth in front of altars: On the end (left in photograph), a figure of a nude one-legged and one-armed man (dark brown) has a pipe (?) in his mouth, and a stem ending in a bowl joined on to the back of his head like a pigtail; this is probably the figure of a sky-deity; for above is a rainbow,[7] called among the Ashanti 'The Sky god's bow',[8] and below it to the right is a cresent moon

---

[1] Description given, regarding an object similarly represented, by J. W. Scott Macfie, *Man*, Nov. 1913, No. 96.

[2] See notes, Pl. IV.

[3] P. A. Talbot, *Southern Nigeria*, vol. ii, p. 104.

[4] R. S. Rattray, *Ashanti Proverbs*, p. 70.

[5] Cf. A. le Herissé, op. cit., Pl. xx.

[6] Ibid.

[7] A rainbow deity is represented on the Palace bas-reliefs at Abomey, E. G. Waterlot, op. cit., Pl. ixa.

[8] R. S. Rattray, *Religion and Art in Ashanti*, p. 174 and Fig. 74.

—Oshu, the moon, was one of the Yoruba minor deities[1]—with a ladder reaching towards it; adjoining the latter is a pair of implements each ending in a forked blade (one being broken off) possibly flutes;[2] behind the figure's feet is a hoe (?). On the rear side (not shown in Plate), a white cock with long bent legs has a hen standing on its back; behind the latter is a tortoise (with dark brown shell); cocks and tortoises are sometimes combined as sacrifices,[3] and the latter is said to typify femininity;[4] below the tortoise is a snail (with yellow shell); behind the cock is a bow fitted with an arrow pointing upwards; above it is a pair of pegs with pierced holes at the top, and a long curved weapon (?). On the rear end (not shown in photograph) there is a series of objects which may be intended to symbolize the deity Shango, God of thunder, namely a blacksmith's tongs, poker, and two anvils, and a curved spiral horn.

The divinities mentioned above are earth and sky gods of the Yoruba-Dahomey religion, of which the figures on the lid are probably emblems, those of the sides depicting their worship or sacrifice for which the vessel was undoubtedly used.

PLATE XXIV
TWO STOOLS

'White' stool (below in photograph).

    Wood; H. (ends) 14¾"; W. (ends) 13¼"; L. (base) 22½".

    Stated to have been 'obtained in King Prempeh's Palace', Ashanti tribe, Gold Coast.

    British Museum, 1896. (Collected during the Ashanti Expedition, 1896.)

The stool is carved from a single piece of light-coloured wood, the material being taken from one or other of two particular species the spirits of which had been propitiated.[5]

The parts forming the seat and the base, as distinct from the central design, are carved in the form invariably used for Ashanti stools, in which the seat is shaped narrower at the centre than at each end, with knobs underneath, known as the ears of the stool.[6] The centre part, forming the support of the seat, is carved in a design of a particular type appropriate to the kind of stool intended, and to the class or sex to which the owner belonged. Its design is not precisely like any of those in the series illustrated by R. S. Rattray,[7] but it is probably of the same type as one called *kotoko gwa*, meaning porcupine stool, reserved to the use of members of the King's

---

[1] P. A. Talbot, *Southern Nigeria*, vol. ii, p. 30.

[2] J. W. Scott Macfie, op. cit.

[3] P. A. Talbot, *In the Shadow of the Bush*, p. 55.

[4] *Southern Nigeria*, vol. ii, p. 83.

[5] R. S. Rattray, *Religion and Art in Ashanti*, p. 271.

[6] R. S. Rattray, *Ashanti*, p. 110.

[7] *Religion and Art in Ashanti*, p. 272.

Council, and also resembles one, called the circular rainbow stool, reserved for the King's use. In either case the design is one exclusively used for persons of the highest rank at Court.

The design includes a column in the centre, which is hollow and carved with a perforated design. An Ashanti carver of stools who was asked by Mr. George Stevens what such patterns signified, said they represented animals or plants, as, for example, the snake or the palm-leaf. On the centre of the seat is fastened a sheet of silver with a curvilinear *repoussé* design, and a band of the same metal is fastened round one leg (not visible in the photograph).

The stool is shown in the Plate lying on one side, the position in which a stool is usually placed by its owner when not in use; the purpose of doing so is to prevent wandering spirits from sitting on it and causing the person who sits there afterwards to contract pains in his waist.[1]

The stool was probably carved at the village of Afwia, a few miles from Coomassie, which, according to Rattray,[2] was the chief centre of the stool-carving industry. Many precautions would have had to be observed before it was carved; when starting to use the tools a rite had to be performed, with wine and the blood of a fowl poured on them, and prayers made for assistance; the carver had to take careful note whether his wife was unfaithful to him, otherwise 'his tools would cut him severely'; work could not be continued if any quarrel at home was left unsettled or there was grievance with the parents.[2]

The stool is said to have been obtained during the Ashanti Expedition of 1896. In the ordinary course of events it would not have been parted with, but would ultimately, on the death of its owner—either King Prempeh (Agyeman) himself or a member of his court—have become a 'blackened' stool, or shrine. The normal course was, however, averted by the unexpected events of 1896, by which the palace was ransacked and the King and all his family sent into exile. It must have been collected from the palace while King Prempeh and his people were, according to W. W. Claridge,[3] assembled at the parade ground for the palaver with the British Governor from the coast. Before this palaver had concluded wending its way towards its inevitable and disastrous conclusion, two companies of the West Yorks, according to the same author, marched down to seize the palace, 'but very little of real value was found'. There was also another palace of the King, from which the stool may have been taken, namely the Summer Palace, which 'was then visited, for it was thought that many of his valuables might have been stored there, but the troops found nothing but a litter of rubbish and rifled boxes'.

[1] R. S. Rattray, *Ashanti Proverbs*, p. 109.   [3] *A History of the Gold Coast and Ashanti,*
[2] *Religion and Art in Ashanti*, p. 271.   London, 1915, vol. ii, p. 411.

'Blackened' stool (above in photograph).

> Wood; H. (ends) 10½"; W. 9⅜"; L. (base) 18".
> Ashanti tribe, Gold Coast.
> *British Museum*, 1896. (Probably collected during the Ashanti Expedition, 1896.)

This stool is carved out of a single piece of light-coloured wood, like the preceding one, which it resembles in style and construction, except in so far as it is consistently smaller, and is without the additional silver decoration.

The particular type of stool to which it belongs is indicated by the design of the central part, consisting of four pillars surrounding a central column perforated with small rectangular holes. This design is one which is more commonly adopted than any other; it is, according to Rattray's[1] list the *'mma gwa*, meaning woman's stool, usually presented by the husband on marriage.

Originally the stool, when it was in use during the lifetime of its owner, was light coloured, like the other. The 'blackening' process would have taken place after her death. This process has left a thick impasto entirely covering it, particularly on the central perforated column, which is partly covered (on the side not shown in the photograph) with a large piece of orange-coloured skin sticking to it. The latter is probably the omentum or covering of fat on the lower intestines of a sacrificed sheep, which, according to Rattray,[2] is part of the offerings placed thus at certain particular functions, known as the 'Wednesday *Adae* ceremonies'; these offerings remain upon the stools till evening, when they are removed, 'the apron of fat alone being left'.

The materials which are used for blackening the stool are generally soot,[2] or a concoction of sooty spiders' webs,[3] mixed with yolk of egg. When the stool has thus become a black one, it is no longer used for sitting on but is deposited in the stool house as an ancestral shrine and treasured heirloom of the clan. The aim of this function is stated by Captain Rattray[2] as follows: 'The stool, which during the lifetime of its possessor was so intimately bound (literally and metaphorically speaking) with its owner's *sunsum* or soul, thus becomes after death a shrine into which the departed spirit may again be called upon to enter on certain special occasions. . . .'

There are no recorded details attached to this stool except the date 1896, which indicates that it must have been obtained under the same circumstances as the preceding specimen. As it appears to have been used very considerably in the

---

[1] *Religion and Art in Ashanti*, pp. 272, 273.   [3] R. S. Rattray, *Ashanti Proverbs*, p. 109.
[2] *Ashanti*, p. 92.

process of ancestor-worship indicated above, it must undoubtedly have been obtained in the course of ransacking one of the sacred stool houses. R. S. Rattray gives vivid descriptions of these, as a result of his being privileged to witness certain religious ceremonies in connexion with them. On the occasion of a *Wukudae* ceremony on the 17 August 1921, he informs us:[1] 'We all entered a very small room, so dark, however, that I could not at first distinguish anything. . . . The chief and all present were dressed in their oldest cloths. . . . He greeted the spirits, saying: *Nananom Samanfo makye o* ('Spirit Grand-fathers, good-morning'). He then seated himself upon his stool. As soon as my eyes grew accustomed to the light, I saw at one end of the room, opposite to the door, a long low platform, raised about three feet off the ground, made of upright poles with cross sticks laid upon them. Upon this table or rack were set the ancestral stools, as yet invisible, for all were covered with one large coarsely woven native cloth called *nsa*. The head stool-carrier came forward and removed the covering. There were thirteen blackened stools, many crumbling to pieces with age. Each stool lay upon its side, the seat facing towards us. They were caked with clotted blood, and pieces of fat could be seen round the centre supports of many of them. The thirteen stools were in three rows. Two brass bells were the only other contents of the room.'

PLATE XXV

GOURDS AND BASKET TRAY

Hanging vessel with designs representing an elephant hunt (top in photograph).

Gourd; H. 15"; Diam. 10".

No recorded provenance.

Probably Kongo tribe, Loanda province, Angola.

British Museum, 1855; given by the Admiralty (Museum of Haslar Hospital).

The gourd has a small opening at the top, and a fibre sling for suspending it, the design being engraved with white lines, and parts stained dark brown. It is an old specimen; it formerly belonged to the Admiralty, and was probably collected by one of the naval expeditions which surveyed the lower Congo. The most likely is that of Captain Tuckey who observed at Noki in 1816 similar gourds used among the Kongo tribe for collecting palm-wine.[2] The design on the bowl consists of hunting scenes which include antelope, snake and elephant, the latter being the chief quarry for the sake of its tail, which is depicted in exaggerated proportions. The

[1] *Ashanti*, p. 95.

[2] *Narrative of an Expedition to Explore the River Zaire*, London, 1818, p. 199.

scene accords closely with accounts of the Kongo people—a name meaning Hunter[1]
—particularly those of the Portuguese Duarte Lopez in 1591. 'Their hunstmen',
he says,[2] 'lie in wait for the elephants as they ascend narrow and steep paths, going
behind them, and with sharp knives cutting off their tails'.

The design appears to be a pictographic record of an actual hunt led perhaps by
the King in person. The part shown in the Plate depicts the start; three huntsmen
(extreme top right) creep forward in single file carrying *dane* guns. The first
creature is a python (centre) hiding by a rock (?) which is shown near its head; it
is killed apparently by the spear thrust from behind. Further on a crouching figure
with a long knife stalks an antelope hiding in the bush—presuming the latter to be
the meaning of the rosettes each side. It is probably the duiker which, Lopez informs us,[3] they hunt cautiously with guns and arrows for the sake of its skin.
Among the next group of figures (partly hidden by the string) appears the leader
(in centre) crouching with hand to mouth, perhaps whistling, and holding aloft a
biforked flag, as used by the King: meanwhile a figure lower down makes a detour,
creeping on all fours with a bow. In front of them (extreme edge) a gun lies upside
down; this is the first hint of tragedy disclosed beyond: the elephant (not visible in
the Plate), attacked in a rocky defile, has seized an assailant in his trunk. While
the victim whistles for help, others attack with gun and knives, and another is
shown approaching from the rear to cut off the animal's coveted tail.

Bottle for containing palm-wine (right in photograph).

> Gourd; H. 12½"; Diam. 6".
> Stated to be 'from Adeeyah (Bubi) tribe, Island of Fernando Po'.
> *Southwark, Cuming Museum,* 1828.

The surface of the gourd is quite plain without any decoration. Its colour resembles
deep mahogany (dark burnt sienna). There is no stopper to the bottle.

There is an inscription pasted on it, which is written in old handwriting and
reads as follows: 'Bottle formed of a gourd for holding "*Topay*" palm wine, Adeeyah
tribe, Island of Fernando Po Africa 1828.' This early date shows that the bottle
was collected in the pioneer days of African exploration and before the period of
European influence in the design of African utensils. It coincides with the date of
the Naval Survey expedition under Captain Owen which formed a settlement at
Fernando Po in 1827, and the bottle was very probably collected by a member of
this party. Having regard to its exceptional elegance in design makes it hard to

---

[1] Sir H. Johnston, *George Grenfell and the Kongo*, vol. i, p. 69.
[2] Filipo Pigafetta, *A Report of the Kingdom of Congo*, Rome 1591 (trans. M. Hutchinson, London, 1881, p. 45).
[3] Op. cit., p. 51.

agree with the impression recorded by one of the party[1] regarding this people, as 'having every requisite accomplishment to entitle them to the name of "Savage" in its most comprehensive sense; in fact, most of the inhabitants of the continent were *gentlemen* of courtly manners and appearance, compared with these unwashed Islanders'.

The name 'Adeeyah', given as the tribal provenance of this bottle, is incorrectly applied to the Fernando Po natives, according to Dr. Baikie[2] who met them in 1854, being a term used to designate the white people, whereas they call themselves Bubi, meaning 'friend'. Dr. Baikie learnt that the palm-wine, for which the bottle is said to be used, is one of the many products which the Bubi derive from the oil-palm tree, being made from its exuded juice.[3] Further information desired by Dr. Baikie was obstructed by a naïve sense of bureaucratic caution, the Bubi chief declaring that should Dr. Baikie wish 'to know more of them, that he would some day call a meeting of chiefs of villages, and ask them to take the matter into consideration'.

The bottle is remarkable for its perfect symmetry and gradation, considering that this effect can only be obtained by carefully influencing its growth. The method is probably like that given in the familiar description in *Swiss Family Robinson*:[4]

'It is the practice of the savages, who have no knives, to use a sort of string, made from the bark of trees, for this purpose.'

'But how can they make bottles,' said he (Fritz).

'That requires some preparation,' replied I. 'They tie a bandage round the young gourd near the stalk, so that the part at liberty expands in a round form, and the compressed part remains narrow. They then open the top, and extract the contents by putting in pebbles and shaking it. By this means they have a complete bottle.'

Ladle with hooked handle (centre in photograph).

> Gourd; H. 9"; W. 4½"; D. 6".
> Stated to be 'from Old Calabar'.
> Probably Efik (Calabaros) tribe, SE. Nigeria.
> *British Museum*, acquired previous to the twentieth century.

The ladle is formed from a gourd cut in half, of which the curved neck forms the handle (only the back appearing in the photograph). The colour is bright orange,

---

[1] *Journal of an Officer*, London, 1833, p. 237.
[2] *Narrative of an Exploring Voyage*, London, 1856, p. 343.
[3] Op. cit., p. 342.
[4] London, ed. 1861, p. 27.

and the design, which is engraved on it, is thinly painted black in a curvilinear style characteristic of the art of the Calabar region. The inside is plain.

The period when it was collected was probably about the middle of last century, judging by its appearance and the handwriting on its label, a time when Old Calabar, or Duke-town, was an important centre for vessels trading with the Efik people.

Bottle with a stopper and very small aperture (left in photograph).

Gourd; H. 9″; Diam. 6″.
Upper Mendi tribe, Sierra Leone.
Brighton Public Museum, either 1899 or 1904. (Collected by T. J. Alldridge.)

The colour of the gourd is light orange (bright yellow ochre). The design is engraved and the lines filled in with white; it is divided into two portions, one on each side, consisting of a series of triangles fitted together.

Small bowl decorated with figures (lower right in photograph).

Gourd; H. 3″; Diam. 6″.
No recorded provenance.
Probably Fanti tribe, Gold Coast.
Newbury Museum.

The bowl[1] is formed from a gourd cut in half. The colour of the gourd, which is not old, is very light brown (pale yellow ochre). The decoration is engraved and the lines filled with white paint.

The bowl is one of a pair, both very similar except in the decorative details. The design consists of a series of symbolic figures: in the centre is a star; round the side is a tree (partly showing on the extreme left in the photograph), from whose branches a large snake appears to be descending; adjoining the tree is a sword of the Ashanti type *afona*,[2] which generally has a gold-covered handle and is used ceremonially. The head of the snake separates two animals, apparently of the cat tribe; that on the left is undoubtedly a lion, while the other, with its claws, fur-markings, and pointed nose is probably the civet or bush cat. These two animals shown in close association may be intended to illustrate the Ashanti proverb[3]: 'Even when a lion is not a strong lion, it is not called a civet cat!' Despite the relative proportions of the two animals as rendered here, the saying is intended to emphasize disproportionate differences in size and strength. Below the civet is a tortoise or else a

---

[1] Cf. two very similar specimens in the Pitt-Rivers Museum, Oxford (no tribal provenance given).

[2] R. S. Rattray, *Religion and Art in Ashanti*, p. 281.

[3] R. S. Rattray, *Ashanti Proverbs*, p. 61.

turtle (known in West Africa as sea-tortoise); if the latter, which it more closely resembles, the provenance of the gourd would be the coastal Fanti rather than the inland Ashanti. A large cross intervenes between the last-mentioned animals and two female figures holding a ladder between them; one of these figures (partly visible on the extreme right in the photograph) has hair in the form of two upright horns, perhaps an exaggerated rendering of the Fanti women's mode of dressing the hair[1]; her right hand holds aloft an object which appears to be a comb; the adjoining figure holds aloft, in a similar manner, a long *dane* gun. Farther round (not visible in the photograph) are a chicken, a flag, and a pair of fetters, a utensil associated in the Ashanti mind with the idea of binding.[2] The latter device, together with several of the others mentioned above, are painted on the Temple walls of the god Ta Kora at Tekiman in northern Ashanti, but according to the priest had no special significance being done according to the fancy of the bricklayer.[2] Possibly the same explanation would be given by the artist of this arrangement of figures. They are probably symbols having a recognized meaning, but perhaps not present in the artist's conscious mind, and consequently arranged according to fancy.

That the bowl is of Gold Coast work is confirmed by comparison with some similar, but older, bowls in Bankfield Museum, Halifax, which contain some of the same devices together with the unmistakable representation of an Ashanti stool. It is difficult to determine to which tribe to assign it, owing to the close cultural association between the two chief groups, Fanti and Ashanti, but considerations founded on general grounds and style of work points to the former of the two as the more probable provenance of the bowl.

Small bottle with a stopper, and decoration derived from string binding (lowest in photograph).

 Gourd; H. 6½″; Diam. 4″.
 Stated to be 'from Western Africa'.
 Probably Zulu or neighbouring tribe, South Africa.
 Southwark, Cuming Museum, about middle of nineteenth century.
The colour of the gourd, which is undoubtedly an old one, is deep orange, and the decoration, which is heavily engraved, is stained or painted black. The design is probably derived from the imitation of string binding in the form of a sling such as is frequently employed in carrying gourds or pots. The stopper is of leather and was probably attached by grass cord passed through a hole in the side of the neck.

An inscription on a label, pasted on the side of the vessel, reads: 'Bottle formed of a gourd, Western Africa'. Its old style of handwriting confirms the probability

---

  [1] Cf. Pl. XII.   [2] R. S. Rattray, *Ashanti*, p. 173.

that the vessel was collected not later than the middle of last century, and from one of the less remote regions known at that time.

Though the ascription to West Africa was accepted as grounds for including the bottle in this series of illustrations, further inspection casts doubts upon the correctness of the label. In shape the gourd closely resembles those of South African tribes; furthermore, in Bankfield Museum, Halifax, there is one almost exactly similar, about a century old, described as a 'Drinking Bottle, Natal'.

Basket tray for sifting meal.
    Cane; Diam. $17\frac{1}{2}''$; D. $2''$.
    Stated to be 'from Bihe'.
    Probably Bihe tribe, Benguella Province, Angola.
    British Museum, acquired previous to 1900.

The tray consists of a rim of wood and strips of cane which are interwoven and fastened to it. The pattern is formed in the weaving; the strips lying in one direction being the natural light colour of the cane (pale yellow ochre), while the strips in the contrary direction are dark brown (sepia).

The material employed is probably the thin split midribs of the palm leaflets, according to J. J. Monteiro's description[1] of a 'Sieve in the form of an open-work basket' in use among the natives of Loanda, and called *uzanzo*.

That the Bihe women also use such trays as this specimen is indicated by an old engraving which depicts one used by a Bihe woman while others are engaged in pounding meal; it is described by Major Serpa Pinto,[2] as a 'Sieve for drying rice'. According to Monteiro,[1] 'the women sift mandioca, Indian corn, or whatever else they may pound into meal in their wooden mortars'; he also says they sift the roots of cassava to make white flour.

The nature of these food-stuffs adds, however, an element of complication as regards the origin of the tray or its style or type of work; for none of these foods were known in this region before the arrival of the Portuguese[3] but are said to have been cultivated there only since their importation, chiefly from Brazil. The foods previously cultivated or eaten—plantains, fungi, fish, and human flesh, &c.—were not such as required the use of a sieve; the use of the latter in this part of Africa must therefore be of comparatively recent origin. Nor is it necessarily of Biheno invention, these people, according to Major Pinto,[4] being 'little given to agriculture or to any kind of manual labour'. Moreover they had every opportunity to borrow or copy

[1] *Angola and the River Congo*, 1875, pp. 88, 287, 304.
[2] Quoted in *Africa and its Exploration*, p. 498.
[3] Sir H. Johnston, *George Grenfell and the Congo*, vol. i, p. 78.
[4] Op. cit., p. 489.

71

it from elsewhere, for they are 'fond of travelling, their roaming disposition being probably due to their origin, as their forefathers came from distant parts'.

One cannot help being struck by the similarity in style of work between the tray and the native Indian work of the Amazon and Orinoco regions. A sieve or tray, which the writer collected at Caicara on the River Orinoco, of Arawak Indian workmanship, closely resembles it in size, circular shallow shape, pattern of dark and light strips and method of weaving, and is moreover similarly used for sifting cassava for making flour. It is reasonable to suppose that such utensils were carried to Africa from Brazil and the Guianas from time to time with the foods for which they were used, and may thus have been met with by the wandering Bihenos, and so borrowed and ultimately copied: somewhat similar trays found in regions much farther east may have had a similar origin.

If this surmise should be correct we have in this tray an exceptional example for comparison between the work of the primitive people of both continents; the Bihe treatment in comparison with that of the Indian being of the two the bolder, the more formulated, but perhaps less refined and graceful.

PLATES XXVI, XXVII, XXVIII
MUSICAL INSTRUMENTS

Harp in the form of a woman standing on an oval base (Plates XXVI and XXVII).
Wood; painted; H. 31½″; W. 8″; D. 6″.
Stated to be 'made by the Varama tribe in the French Congo; obtained at Sette Cama'.
Probably Commi (Nkomi) tribe, Gabun.
Liverpool Free Public Museum, 1904.

The harp is constructed in two pieces and includes an arm or neck and a sound-box. The former is of hard wood, secured to the neck of the figure with cane binding; and has eight wooden pegs for tuning. The latter is formed by the hollow body of the figure, 3½″ deep, and covered with a piece of thin skin bound round it with fibre-string. The skin is probably that of either a gazelle or goat[1]; and the strings, which are eight in number, are of vegetable growth, probably the fine fibrous roots of the palm tree[1], which, according to T. E. Bowdich, are very tough and not apt to slip.[2]

The figure is carved from light-coloured wood entirely covered with paint, the colours being as follows: neck and face, white; hair, lips, and eyebrows, dark brown (sepia); the rest of the figure including a band across the bridge of the nose and

[1] P. du Chaillu, *Adventures in Equatorial Africa*, London, 1861, p. 391.
[2] *Sketch of Gabun*, London, 1819, p. 450.

round the eyes, red (orange-vermilion). The eyes consist of pieces of white glazed pottery with black centres; and each ear has a wire ring suspended from it.

The hair, in the form of a high bunch, represents a style of hairdressing—generally puffed out on a framework of leaves or other material—which is characteristic of several of the Gabun tribes, but, judging by sketches reproduced by Du Chaillu, most closely resembles that worn by the 'Mpongwe and the Commi (Nkomi, Camma)[1] tribes. The resemblance in the case of the latter people is also enforced by the wire rings they wear in their ears; and furthermore it is they who occupy the coastal region around Sette Cama, whence the harp was collected. Its provenance therefore may be safely ascribed to the Commi, of whom the Varama—the provenance named on the label of the harp, but unidentified—are probably a part.

The colours, red and white, with which the figure is painted, are said to be connected with spirits or ghosts; and are used by members of the secret societies, such as *Bouiti*[2] among the men and *Njembe*[3] among the women, for painting themselves when attending their religious ceremonies. Probably the figure depicts a woman, thus richly decorated, engaged in dances at which the harp itself might be played.

Its form differs from that of the modern European instrument by the absence of the front pillar, but resembles the ancient Egyptian harp. According to Du Chaillu[4] this type of harp has the same name *ombi* as the 'banjo or guitar'; his experience of its playing results in the following observation; 'Often and often I have heard it played all night, while the crowd of listeners sat in silence round the fire. While the tom-tom rouses their feelings, and really throws them into a frenzy, the *ombi* has a soothing and softening effect upon them.'

T. E. Bowdich[5] ventures upon comparisons with Handel in his response to a 'Mpongwe performance on the harp in 1817. The player and singer whom he heard was a 'white' negro from the interior country of Imbeekee; his eyes were 'small, bright, and of a dark grey; the light seemed to hurt them; and their constant quivering and rolling gave his countenance an air of insanity. He sat on a low stool, and supporting his harp on his knee and shoulder, proceeded to tune it with great nicety; his hands seemed to wander amongst the strings until he gradually formed a running accompaniment (but with little variety) to his extraordinary vociferations. At times, one deep and hollow note burst forth and died away; the sounds of the harp became broken; presently he looked up, pursuing all the actions of a maniac, taking one hand from the strings, to wave it up and down, stretching forth one leg,

---

[1] Op. cit., pp. 6, 196.
[2] P. Daney, 'Sur les croyances des indigènes de la Subdivision de Sindara', *Revue anthropologique*, 1924, pp. 278–80.
[3] J. L. Wilson, *Western Africa*, New York, 1856, pp. 396–7. See also Pl. XIX.
[4] Op. cit., p. 391.
[5] Op. cit., p. 450.

L

and drawing it up again as if convulsed, lowering the harp on to the other foot, and tossing it up and down. Whilst the one hand continued playing, he rung forth a peal which vibrated on the ear long after it had ceased; he was silent; the running accompaniment served again as a prelude to a loud recitative, uttered with the greatest volubility, and ending with one word, with which he ascended and descended, far beyond the extent of his harp, with the most beautiful precision. Sometimes he became more collected, and a mournful air succeeded the recitative, though without the least connexion, and he would again burst out with the whole force of his powerful voice in the notes of the "Hallelujah" of Handel. To meet with this chorus in the wilds of Africa, and from such a being, had an effect I can scarcely describe, and I was lost in astonishment at the coincidence. There could not be a stronger proof of the nature of Handel or the powers of the negro.'

Harp with decoration in the form of a person's head (Plates XXVI and XXVII).

    Wood; H. 31"; W. 4"; D. 4½".
    No recorded provenance.
    Probably Bakalai or neighbouring tribe, Gabun.
    British Museum, 1870.

This harp has eight strings and is constructed in a similar manner to the preceding one. The wood is painted black, but has a shiny surface, apparently due to being varnished—possibly since acquisition. The piece of animal's skin which covers the hollow sound-box has fur of reddish-brown colour, probably that of a goat.

    The only information accompanying this harp is inscribed on an old label, which states that its provenance is from 'the interior of Africa'. It is undoubtedly from the Gabun region. In shape it closely resembles a harp of the Bakalai tribe, illustrated by Du Chaillu.[1] Harps from the Gabun usually have the upper part carved in the form of the head of a human being. The head depicted in this harp has a head-dress hanging down behind, intended either for a cap of the Loango type[2] or for a mode of hairdressing.

Harp-guitar, decorated with four figures sitting and kneeling and one standing (Plates XXVI and XXVIII).

    Wood; H. 33"; W. (box) 5½"; D. (box) 4½".
    No recorded provenance.
    Probably Chekiani or neighbouring tribe, Gabun.
    British Museum, no date, probably third quarter of nineteenth century.

The colour of the wood is light, tanned to that of dark orange; there are traces of

---

[1] *Adventures in Equatorial Africa*, p. 294.   [2] Like a 'night-cap', worn by men of rank.

paint—vermilion and blue—in the incised lines on the sound-box, and two of the figures are painted black.

This form of harp differs from that of the preceding types. It consists of a hollow sound-box covered with a piece of wood fastened with brass-headed nails, and an arm or bow consisting of five reeds which are bound together with cane and fastened to the back of the sound-box. The strings, which are thin fibrous tree roots, as in the preceding harps, are five in number, attached to the separate tips of each reed, the natural spring of which is sufficient to keep them taut.

Both sides of the sound-box are decorated with a carved incised pattern. The figures on the top of the box include two who are represented squatting on their heels, with hands folded across the chest, and two who are sitting. Brass buttons are used to depict the navel; circular pieces of white shell with black centres and edges are used for the eyes, as in the first harp. The smaller figure, standing on a circular base, is intended for the guardian divinity. It has, on the middle of its body, a lump of resin with a shell in the centre, and an orange-vermilion feather stuck upright in it. The shininess of the former and colour of the latter enable it to ward off hostile spirits. The figures are evidence that the guitar is from Gabun.

Paul du Chaillu,[1] describing an instrument of this type with sound-box similarly decorated, names it the '*wambee*: The Shekiani banjo'; the Shekiani being a semi-nomadic tribe dwelling mostly near the 'Mpongwe and the Bakalai. T. E. Bowdich,[2] writing of the 'Mpongwe, names it 'the *enchambee*' and describes its playing as follows: 'It is played with both hands; the tones are sweet, but have little power or variety. Long stories are recited to the *enchambee* in the moonlight evenings, in a sort of recitative; a favourite one is an account of the acts by which the sun gained the ascendancy over the moon, who were first made of coeval power by their common father.' The author mentions two songs played with this instrument; one commences, he imagines, in F major and ends in G major: 'A native envies a neighbour, named Engaella who has ivory to barter with a vessel.' Another, 'in G major, is a song in which the men sing the air alone, and the women join in the chorus. It is an old one, and the subject the first appearance of a white man.'

Fiddle with gourd resonator (Plate XXVI, bottom of photograph).

Wood and gourd; L. 22½″; H. (gourd) 7″.

Probably Basonge (Basanga) tribe, Belgian Congo.

British Museum. (Probably collected by E. Torday, 1907–9.)

This instrument consists of a half-gourd as resonator, with a separate cap, also of gourd, and an arm of wood; these are fastened together by means of sinnet bound to

[1] *Adventures in Equatorial Africa*, p. 163.   [2] *A Sketch of Gabun*, 1819, p. 449.

a wooden peg fitted across the neck of the gourd inside. The arm has three fibre strings with a bridge at one end made of cane and fastened also with sinnet.

The gourd is decorated with a pattern of black incised lines and brass-headed nails. There is also a cord strung with blue beads which enables the instrument to be suspended from a person's shoulder.

This instrument is probably the one collected by Emil Torday from the Basonge tribe during his 1907–9 Congo Expedition, and which he describes in collaboration with T. A. Joyce in the *Annales du Musée du Congo belge*[1] as a 'Guitare Basonge', a type probably introduced to these people from elsewhere.

The distribution of this form of instrument is very wide—as far north as the Aruwimi in the Belgian Congo,[2] and as far south as the Awemba in Northern Rhodesia.[3] This specimen is probably based on an Awemba model, judging by the brass-headed nail decoration of the gourd.

The Basonge are said to be very keen musicians. M. W. Hilton-Simpson[4] considers, judging by a concert to which he and Torday listened, that the Basonge are unrivalled as instrumental musicians: 'So exactly did they keep time and come in at the right moment that the melody produced was extremely pleasing to the European ear.'

War gong (Plate XXVI, right background in photograph).
    Iron; H. 38″; W. (base) 14¾″; D. (base) 4½″.
    Stated to be 'from Compound of Kefi, Nasarawa Province'.
    Probably Guari tribe, Northern Nigeria.
    British Museum, 1907.

This instrument is made out of a piece of beaten iron, including the three flat pieces, one in front of each other, with iron rings suspended from the edges. The circular disk at the top, however, with rings hanging round the edge, is a separate piece, fitted on.

The gong is lozenge-shaped in its section, similar to the small iron gongs which are played while held in the hand. It is probably used by means of a beater, which causes the rings to make a jangling sound.

It is stated to be 'probably old Guari work', namely a scattered tribe who range towards Bornu.[5]

[1] 'Notes ethnographiques', Brussels, 1922, p. 24 and Fig. 10.

[2] Sir H. Johnston, *George Grenfell and the Congo*, vol. ii, Fig. 389.

[3] E. W. Smith and A. M. Dale, *The Ila-speaking Peoples of Northern Rhodesia*, London, 1920, vol. ii, p. 262.

[4] *Land and Peoples of the Kasai*, pp. 35, 36.

[5] O. Temple, *Notes on the Tribes, etc., of the Northern Provinces of Nigeria*, Capetown, 1919, p. 120.

Drum (Plate XXVI, left background in photograph).

> Wood and skin; H. 11¾″; Diam. 16½″.
> Stated to be 'from West Africa'.
> *Royal United Services Museum*, probably acquired about 1874.

The drum is carved out of wood, with the drum-head covered with animal skin. The latter is held tightly in place by means of leathern thongs joining the edge of the membrane to the base of the drum where they are passed round a wooden ring on which it stands, the ends being then rejoined to the membrane. The drum is thus encased in a net. Several wooden pegs provide additional means of tightening the skin.

The drum is described as 'a war drum', probably due to its having been obtained in the course of some military expedition. It was one of the early possessions of the old United Services Museum, and there is no record of its exact provenance, which is difficult to ascertain, but is probably Southern Nigeria, judging by the type and date of acquisition.

When played, the drum would be placed upright on the ground and not carried, and probably beaten with the hand and fingers.

P. A. Talbot[1] states from his own experiences in Nigeria that 'the monotonous "tom-toming" goes to the heads of the people and produces a kind of semi-intoxication'; but its musical value is indicated by 'the extraordinary amount of feeling which can be put into it, the great variety of tunes and the skilfulness with which they are played', which 'seem to vibrate on chords of being which more strictly beautiful performances fail to touch'.

Cloth decorated with 'stylized' figures (Plate XXVI).

> Woven cotton; L. 78½″; W. 49″.
> Stated to be 'made at Jellah Coffee, Gold Coast'.
> Probably Awuna tribe, Jelakofi, Gold Coast.
> *Liverpool, Free Public Museum*, 1907.

This cloth is woven on a 'narrow-band' loom[2] in twelve vertically placed strips. The colours used are white, black, and deep red (scarlet), the tone showing darkest being black with red edge, the lighter tone being a mixture of black and white threads, and the background being white only.

The pattern is in five horizontal bands, of which the central one includes stylized figures of two human beings and two animals. One of these is probably intended for either a turtle or tortoise, judging by the bird's-eye view of it and the bend back-

---

[1] *Southern Nigeria*, vol. iii, pp. 809, 811   [2] See notes, Pl. VI.

wards of the legs or flippers and despite its long tail; and the other a civet cat, judging by its sharp nose pointed downwards, straight tail, and absence of horns or prominent ears.

PLATE XXIX

CEREMONIAL HOE, HEAD-RESTS, AND RITUAL BOWL

Ceremonial hoe consisting of the figure of a one-legged man carrying a bird on his back.

> Hard wood and iron; H. 13″; W. (centre) 2¼″; D. (head) 2½″.
> Stated to be 'from Bakongo tribe', Kasai region, Belgian Congo.
> *British Museum*, 1910. (Collected by E. Torday.)

The colour of the wood is very dark brown (sepia), probably darkened with age, and the surface is thickly incrusted. The figure of the man is depicted nude, with two horns representing those of the antelope on the back of his head—the farther one of the two is broken off—and a disk projecting from each temple. The back of the neck is decorated with lumps, probably depicting keloids or cicatrices, and between the breasts and the navel there is also a group of four lumps arranged diamond-fashion. The elbows are detached from the body, and the arms are covered with a faint pattern of incised lines; similar lines are also incised on the sides and back of the single thigh. The figure of a bird is shown in an attitude of clinging to the back of the man, with its wings half-closed and beak pointing upwards.

The iron blade, of which one end is held in the mouth of the figure, is decorated with faint incised lines forming a zigzag and diamond pattern.

A note accompanying this specimen describes it as a 'ceremonial hoe, carried on shoulder'. The specimen is also intended to be used as a rake by means of the two horns which 'are used for scraping aside the weeds already removed from the ground'.[1]

A hoe very similar to this one is illustrated by Sir H. Johnston[2] and ascribed to the 'Bapindi (Ba-Pende) tribe'. The same provenance is also given for a comb of similar work in the Philadelphia Museum.[3] The 'Bapindi' provenance is, however, probably incorrect. The carving of the figure shows no resemblances to that of Ba-Pende work. Probably this ascription is due to the close proximity of that tribe to the Ba-Kongo of the Kasai region and intermixture of their respective villages.

---

[1] E. Torday and T. A. Joyce, *J.R.A.I.*, vol. xxxvii, 1907, Pl. xvii.

[2] *George Grenfell and the Congo*, vol. ii, Fig. 23.

p. 625.

[3] *The Museum Journal*, June 1923,

Until Torday's visit to the Ba-Kongo in 1909, the latter were reputed to be inaccessible to white men. Thus earlier examples of Ba-Kongo work, such as those mentioned above, may have been acquired through the Ba-Pende, though their actual provenance was Ba-Kongo.

Head-rest or 'pillow' in the form of a nude female squatting on a high circular base (bottom right in photograph).
>   Hard wood; H. 4¾"; W. 3⅜"; D. (base) 2⅝".
>   Stated to be 'from Zombo tribe', North Angola.
>   *British Museum*, 1905.

The pillow is carved from one piece of dark wood, the colour of raw umber. The figure depicts a nude woman without decoration other than a slight projection in the form of a bun at the back of the head, and sitting on her heels in a squatting position.

Joachim John Monteiro[1] illustrates by a sketch a very similar pillow which he states was brought to the coast by a caravan from Bembe in the neighbourhood of the Zombo country. This possibly explains how such pillows have been obtained by collectors, for the same author also informs us that they are mostly used by the negroes from the interior and are carried with them slung from their shoulder when they travel.

Wooden pillows are chiefly employed to prevent damage to an elaborate coiffure. Their distribution, therefore, naturally follows that of elaborate forms of hairdressing. The form of these pillows, according to Sir Harry Johnston,[2] can be traced to an origin in ancient Egypt.

Head-rest or 'pillow' supported by a two-faced anthropomorphic figure, standing on an oval base, and called '*Kikuma*'.
>   Hard wood; H. 5¾"; W. 10½"; D. (base) 4¾".
>   Stated to be 'from Mossonge, Northern Ba-Mbala tribe', Kwango district, Belgian Congo.
>   *British Museum*, 1907. (Collected by E. Torday.)

The wood is extremely light in colour, equivalent to pale yellow (naples); and the surface is very smooth and neither stained nor painted. The figure, apart from its arms, is repeated so as to face front and back alike.[3] The ear-holes, nostrils, and

---

[1] *Angola and the River Congo*, London, 1875, Pl. iv and p. 284.
[2] *George Grenfell and the Congo*, vol. ii, p. 744.

[3] Cf. another similar specimen, collected at Putumbumba, now in the same collection, ill. *J.R.A.I.*, vol. xxxvii, 1907, Pl. xvii.

toes are blackened, as if they had been charred by a boring instrument. The hair is shown with a curved edge, shaped like a forepeak, representing the fashion worn by the Southern, and parental, branch of the tribe.

Bowl supported on the figure of a kneeling woman on a rectangular base.

Hard wood, carved in one piece; H. 7"; Diam. 5¼".

Stated to be 'from Abomey, Dahomey'.

British Museum, 1889. (Mrs. Turnbull Collection.)

The meagre information supplied by the label of this specimen shows that it was collected at the capital of the old kingdom of Dahomey, and that it was acquired in the year 1889, a date which happens to coincide with that in which the Dahomey King Gelele died. European visitors to this capital were not at any time numerous, but it was customary to attend the ceremonies of the 'Grand Customs', lasting several months, which followed a king's death, and in the course of which great numbers of persons were put to death in order to serve the dead king in the world to follow; and one may surmise that this specimen was collected by a person visiting the capital under these circumstances.

The wood is light coloured (yellow ochre), with a clearly marked grain and very smooth surface, neither stained nor painted; the grain of the wood follows the circle of the bowl, with the core of the wood at the centre.

The bowl has a flat base resembling a basket or basin, resting on the head of the figure, and is 1⅜" deep inside. A band of pattern, consisting of a series of notches, ornaments the upper edge of the bowl and also the base. The figure kneeling, and sitting on the heels, is depicted nude, with the exception of a string of beads encircling the waist, and a necklace of beads containing a locket or charm. The absence of costume, tribal marks, and hairdressing suggests that the figure is intended to represent a slave woman, supporting a basin in the manner usual when fetching water or carrying loads. Possibly the basin is intended for the type used for corn; it may be compared with a very large carving of a kneeling girl carrying a bowl on her head, and of Yoruba origin, which is illustrated by Major A. J. N. Tremearne,[1] who was informed that it was the Goddess of Hunting.

Sacred bowls were much used in connexion with the religious rites of the Oracle of Ife, the Holy City of the Yoruba nation. H. U. Hall[2] mentions figures of this kind, 'bearing on their heads open wooden bowls,' which he states, 'form part of the accessories in Ifa ritual'. The people of Dahomey were in close contact with the Yoruba and the wood carvings of both peoples usually show close resemblances.

[1] *The Tailed Head Hunters of Nigeria,* 1912, p. 34.

[2] *The Museum Journal,* Philadelphia, March, 1917, p. 55.

The figure obviously is intended for use as a receptacle, but there is nothing to indicate definitely its mode of use, which was probably in a religious ceremony corresponding to the Ifa ritual.

Though the carving is obviously related to Yoruba work, it displays the hand of the Dahomey wood-carver in its rounded, rich, but exquisite surface.

PLATE XXX
CANOE PADDLES AND HOE

Large ceremonial paddle with blade in the form of a reptile and with the figure of a snake on the end of the handle (centre in photograph).

Hard wood; painted; L. (total) 85½″, (blade) 38¼″; W. (blade) 9¾″; D. (blade) 2½″.
Stated to be 'from Bonny'.
Probably Kalabari tribe, S. Nigeria.
Liverpool, Free Public Museum. (Collected by Rev. Archdeacon D. C. Crowther, Pastorate Mission, Bonny, 1901.)

The cirumstances in which this paddle was obtained are narrated in a note, written by Archdeacon Crowther, and dated March, 1901, as follows: 'This *juju* is called *Oru*, owned by a man who is a fisherman. He used to consult this *juju* before setting out to fish, and believed that by invoking it he will ensure success. As you see it is in the shape of an alligator, which is the object of worship in that town in the Delta and Bakana. The owner of this *juju* attended our service one day and was so impressed with what he heard, how the God of Heaven is the Creator and dispenser of all things and by Jesus Christ only is salvation. He came again and again, and in a few months he enlisted his name as an adherent of the Church, and before some months more he voluntarily delivered up this *juju* to the agent of the Delta Pastorate station there (Bakana) and is now a candidate for baptism.'

The writer of the above, Archdeacon Crowther, is himself a native of Nigeria, being the son of the celebrated Bishop Samuel Crowther, a Yoruban from the village of Oshugun, who, as a youth, in 1823 was sold to Portuguese slavers, but was rescued and freed by means of a British warship;[1] the mission station at Bonny presided over by Archdeacon Crowther was originally founded on behalf of the Church Missionary Society by the pioneer work of his father.

The blade of the paddle is decorated only on one side, the other side being plain.

[1] Rev. S. Crowther, *Journal of the Niger Expedition of 1841*; Appendix. A number of specimens collected by Bishop Crowther from Nigeria are in the C.M.S. Collection, London.

DESCRIPTION OF PLATES

The figure, depicting a reptile, is carved in high relief, and is painted black and white, including the eyes and teeth; the rest of the head, however, is left the natural brown colour of the wood, resembling ash. The check pattern, in addition to being painted, is carved so that the white squares are sunk below the level of the black ones; the eyes are also carved in relief. The handle, which is round, is quite plain, except at the far end, where there is a figure of a snake, $11\frac{1}{2}''$ in length, also carved in high relief, and painted similarly to the other figure. Portions of the handle have been eaten away by insects—probably white ants—and where the tail of the figure extends up the handle has been repainted with black and white checks over the damaged part, probably while in native use.

The place, Bakana, where the paddle was given up to the mission by its owner, is one of three slave villages recently settled by the Kalabari,[1] a branch of the Ijaw and a very ancient people. Probably the paddle was brought with them when they left Old Shipping (Kalabari) in 1880. As the owner of the paddle is described as a fisherman, it is more than probable that he was a member of this tribe who, according to P. A. Talbot,[2] have devoted themselves to that profession, 'since the stoppage of the slave trade. . . . In this they are greatly helped by their almost entire control of the fishing grounds; for dried fish here, as throughout West Africa, is one of the most highly prized articles of food.' If the paddle is an old one—and it has every appearance of being so—it may have been made before they took to fishing, for a purpose nothing to do with that profession. Such circumstances would prove a very cogent reason why it was considered useless and surrendered to the mission.

In any case the paddle is too large and heavy to be intended for practical use in the water, and must have been meant for purely ceremonial purposes. Some indication of its use is given by a photograph, reproduced by Talbot,[3] showing an altar with two paddles placed on either side of it, described as a class of *juju* named *Ibudu*, whose function is 'protection and bring plenty piccans', the two paddles being 'for the ferrying out and in of souls at birth and death'. If this comparison is correct, the function of the paddle is to assist fertility.

A valuable detail given in the Archdeacon's note is the name *Oru* which he applies to the paddle. This is a term which, according to Talbot's[4] classification, signifies a 'land spirit', as distinct from *Owu Amapo*, meaning 'water spirit'. This distinction adds a complication to the problem of ascertaining the subject of the paddle; for the 'alligator', as the Archdeacon has described the figure, supposing this to mean the West African crocodile, could scarcely be described as a land spirit. But

[1] P. A. Talbot, *The Tribes of the Niger Delta*, London, 1932, p. 8.
[2] Op. cit., p. 9.
[3] Op. cit., p. 94.
[4] Op. cit., p. 32.

the nature of the reptile depicted on the paddle is by no means certain; it appears to have a hybrid identity, for it is shown possessing forelegs bent backwards like those of the tortoise. The crocodile, though regarded as sacred in many parts of South Nigeria,[1] is not specially reported to be so in the region of Bonny. On the other hand, another reptile, whose appearance represented in a carving might be readily confused with that of the crocodile, is the giant lizard called the iguano. This creature is a land reptile whose special cult and sanctity at Bonny has been much noted.[2] In 1825, in consequence of a mate of one of the trading vessels having killed an iguano, all further trade was stopped by orders of King Pebble and his people.[3] Perhaps this is the creature which Archdeacon Crowther means by the term 'alligator', the name of a species which correctly speaking is not native to West Africa but is said to belong to North America and China. The head of the figure is indeed more like that of the crocodile than the iguano, but in other respects it might equally well be the latter creature.

As regards the figure of a snake at the far end of the paddle, its representation is quite consistent with the description and provenance of the paddle, for among the cults practised in the region of Bonny is that of a snake-deity called *Numkpo*, which is said to be a land-spirit.[4]

If the paddle had not an actual record of its provenance, it would have been supposed that it originated from the region of the Cross River, among the Ekoi or the Efik. In that region the cult of the snake is combined with that of the crocodile, as forms adopted by the women's goddess Nimm, representations of both creatures together being found on the walls of Egbo Secret Society houses.[5] Furthermore, in Ekoi art, the black and white check pattern is often employed. On an Ekoi wooden pillar it is used in the representation of a crocodile in a manner closely similar to that of this figure.[6]

If the paddle is not an actual Ekoi work which has drifted to the region where it was found, it is at least probably derived from a source common to both. Such a conclusion might account for the dubious nature of the subject of the paddle; for a representation of a crocodile from a region where that animal is sacred might be subsequently adopted at Bonny as the representation of the sacred iguano and 'land spirit'.

---

[1] A. G. Leonard, *The Lower Niger and its Tribes*, pp. 364, 365.

[2] R. F. Burton, *Wanderings in West Africa*, 1863; Rev. Hope Waddell, *West Indies and Central Africa*, 1863, p. 270.

[3] *Journal of an Officer*, London, 1833, p. 266.

[4] A. G. Leonard, op. cit., p. 354.

[5] P. A. Talbot, *In the Shadow of the Bush*, p. 24.

[6] Op. cit., p. 25.

Canoe paddle with perforated blade, decorated with figures of animals (left in photograph).

Hard wood; painted; L. (whole) 57"; W. (blade) 6"; Diam. (handle) $1\frac{3}{4}$".

Stated to be 'from Jekri tribe, Forcados, S. Nigeria'.

Oxford, Pitt-Rivers Museum. (Collected by C. J. M. Gordon, 1901.)

This paddle is said to have been 'in native use at the time it was collected'. It is carved in one piece, and is entirely covered with paint, the colours being red (scarlet), green (viridian), both of which show as the darker tone, and white, which shows as the lighter tone. The tip of the blade and other parts are green, while the parts which are red include the two uppermost figures of animals. The handle is coloured green, except for the 'hand-grips' at the top and the centre, which are red and white, these being the parts by which the paddle is held when used; that at the top (not visible in the photograph) is shaped like a cone, while that in the centre consists of a rounded handle with a loop carved at each end to resemble the links of a chain. The perforated openings in the blade are said to provide a better grip of the water than a plain surface, according to information given to the writer by the Curator of the Pitt-Rivers Museum (Mr. Henry Balfour, F.R.S.).

The carved patterns and arrangement of colours are not the same on each side of the blade. The four figures representing animals are possibly intended for the chameleon. They are similarly represented in work of the Bini[1] tribe, a people who are said to be kinsmen of the Jekri.[2]

The chameleon is regarded by the Bini as their sign of wisdom.[3] It is said to live close to rivers and streams where the jungle is thick, and is believed by some of the Lower Niger tribes to possess miraculous powers such as rendering itself invisible and detecting the presence of an enemy or a human being.[4] The great value of these qualities from the point of view of a river boatman would account for the representation of this animal on the blade of the paddle, as in the nature of a charm.

Paddles of this type,[5] though used by the Jekris, are, according to the late H. Ling Roth,[6] often made by their neighbours the Ijos, a fishing people. 'The Jekris are a water people who prefer to paddle many miles to walking a few yards. . . . Whole families live in their canoes and travel up and down the river, but always wait for

[1] Cf. an iron staff *ematon*, R. E. Dennett, *At the Back of the Black Man's Mind*, Pl. xvii, p. 194.

[2] A. G. Leonard, *The Lower Niger and its Tribes*, p. 28. A similar paddle in the British Museum is described 'Benin River'.

[3] Dennett, op. cit., p. 194.

[4] Leonard, op. cit., p. 192.

[5] Cf. two similar, but unpainted, examples exhibited in the Fitzroy Tavern, Charlotte Street, London.

[6] 'Notes on the Jekris, Sobos, and Ijos', *J.R.A.I.*, vol. i, 1898, pp. 105, 121; based on a series of Jekri paddles in Bankfield Museum, Halifax.

the tides and are never in a hurry to go anywhere. The chiefs have big canoes with plenty of small boys paddling; these they keep going for sometimes as much as twenty hours at a stretch. The boys often fall asleep and off their seats, and if they do not paddle properly, a man hits them on the head, the boys being generally slaves'.

Canoe paddle decorated with a design representing the face of a clock (bottom of photograph).

> Very hard wood; L. (whole) 58″; W. (blade) 5½″; Diam. (handle) 1¼″.
> Stated to be 'from Sobo tribe, Okitipupa, S. Nigeria'.
> *Oxford, Pitt-Rivers Museum.* (Collected by W. J. W. Norcott, 1931.)

This is said to be 'an old paddle which was still in native use when collected'. It is carved from one piece of wood, which has a very shiny surface and is entirely unpainted, the colour being very dark brown, equivalent to neutralized raw umber. Both sides of the blade are decorated with rectangular bands of 'interlacing' pattern, but the design representing a clock-face appears on one side only, the other side having a diamond-shaped pattern. The designs are carved in low relief, necessitating the laborious work of cutting away the remaining surface. The handle is carved with grooves.

The paddle differs from the type usually employed among the tribes of this region, and of which the preceding figure is a typical example; the difference being chiefly in its heavy wood, blunt tip, and unperforated blade.

Its representation of a clock-face was probably inspired by the wonder and interest which this instrument excited when first displayed; and probably the paddle dates from a period when the clock or watch was still comparatively unfamiliar. Paul du Chaillu[1] narrates—regarding a period so late as 1860—that his clock was thought by the Ashira natives to be his guardian spirit, and its constant ticking to denote its watchfulness. Possibly a similar idea is intended regarding this paddle, namely a vigilant guardianship which would guide the paddle aright and preserve the boatmen from unknown dangers, a function somewhat comparable to that of the chameleon in the preceding figure. The clock carving would thus be considered from the point of view of the boatman as a species of charm.

Three-pronged paddle (right in photograph).

> Hard wood; L. (whole) 52½″; W. (blade) 14½″; Diam. (handle) 2″.
> No recorded provenance; believed to be from Angola.
> Probably Mussorongo (Mucilongo) tribe, Loanda.
> *British Museum,* acquired previous to 1900.

[1] *Adventures in Equatorial Africa*, p. 412.

85

The paddle is carved from one piece of wood, the colour of which is like that of ash; the blade is bevelled towards the edges of each prong.

The paddle belongs to a type which is used in sea-going canoes employed for fishing, and is found in most parts of the west coast. If the provenance of the paddle, uncertainly ascribed to Angola, is correctly given, the tribe from which it was obtained is probably the Mussorongo (Mucilongo), dwelling on the south bank of the Congo River, who are essentially a water people. Northcote Thomas[1] writes of them, in this connexion: 'In their dug-out canoes from ten to forty feet long, they carry their produce to market, or steal silently up a creek to set their fish-traps.'

Throughout the west coast the people most famous as sea-fishermen and boat-men are the Grebo or Kru-boy of the Grain Coast, Liberia. They trade for long distances, and it is possible that the paddle, if not of Grebo origin, is derived from theirs.

The two essays appended below, written by native fishermen of the Gold Coast, describe the tasks for which this paddle would be carved. The glimpse they give into the personal point of view of one of that calling is intended to be the justification for their inclusion here, if not also for their literary and imaginative qualities.

'Being a fisherman's son, it happened one day that some old fishermen, about three in number, who were not at all the sort I was used to, came to tell my father that they want to go fishing to-day, but their number is less of one; so beg him to let me accompany them.

'I was listening all the time, with that respectful consideration one then gave to all grown-up people. My father called me and told me all, but of course I was not present officially, so to speak. I went with them.

'It seemed a serious indictment enough as they rowed the canoe out, for the sea was boisterous. In tact, consideration, as well as in taste and beautiful sensibilities —we failed at every point. We rowed with all our possible best of nature, but all in vain; and I began to feel like collapsing on the carpet from sheer spiritual anaemia. But when one of the elders gave an order in a form of command, and rowed with all his strength and helped by the others in the same manner, in a minute or two we were over the waves. When the sail was hoisted and the canoe was pulling by the wind, my thought reverted somehow to a game we had played a day before. About 12 o'clock in the noon, the bright sun overhead shone upon us all with all its tropical impartiality, and the hungry sharks, whose fins scored the limitless Atlantic by darting on every side, were impelled by an appetite that made no exception as to sex.

'When we shared the ultimate food we had, and circulated the last water-keg, the

---

[1] *Women of all Nations*, 1908, p. 96.

men got an absolute fourth apiece; and neither more nor less, and the only partiality shown was in favour of one man, who was allowed to perceive and to hail saviour-sail on the horizon. And this was only because it was his turn to do so, not because he happened to be this or that. I was thinking whither I should shape my course, and the sort of canoe I should occupy for my next fishing. The canoe was leaking, and the water therein was my duty to carry out, as the middle of the canoe was where I was posted. Out beyond soundings the big waves were racing. We were humming close-hauled, and the shrouds thrilling musically, in much less time. At this critical point in the conflict the boatswain, grasping me by the arm, drew my attention to a mighty canoe on the shore, while the signalman on the shore required us whether we wanted any assistance or preferred to come through the waves with the little job ourselves. And the boatswain replied, We will try; and by the help of the Almighty we came to the shore safely.'[1]

'My future work will be that of a fisherman. Many people will laugh at me when I say this; but they forget that it was and is one of the most primitive works. From it once we got our teachers and expounders of the Gospel—God's own men, and afterwards fishers no more of fishes, but of men. . . . But I ask is it the literate class and the fine arts men of the world alone that do help materially? What about those men that sustain them and keep them going? Alas, my countrymen seem to set their faces against this noble work. . . . England, whom we imitate doggedly to-day on the Gold Coast, has not shunned the fishing work. It is rather being carried on in a grander scale. . . . I do not think I will be jeering at my education when I take up the work of a fisherman, but rather I should think I would be doing her worthy service. I conclude with both joy and hearty laughter that I will be a fisherman when I am a man.'[2]

Hoe.

> Hard wood and iron; L. (handle) $29\frac{1}{2}''$; L. (blade) $25''$; W. (blade) $6''$.
> Stated to be 'Mandingo tribe, Balson, Kombo, Gambia'.
> *Brighton Public Museum*, 1926. (Formerly in the Imperial Institute.)

The wood is grained resembling mahogany, and is unpainted. It consists of two pieces, handle and blade; the former is formed from a forked piece of wood, of which the shorter prong is bevelled to fit in a groove cut in the wooden blade. The two pieces are bound together by means of a very long strip of cane ($\frac{1}{4}''$ wide), passed through holes in the blade and round both prongs of the handle, thus form-

---

[1] From *Our Days on the Gold Coast*, ed. by Lady de Clifford, 1919, p. 96. [2] By a pupil of Government Senior Boys' School, Accra; op. cit., p. 218.

ing an almost solid bar between the two. The cutting-edge of the blade is formed by a piece of iron.

This implement is used, according to R. A. Freeman,[1] 'with one hand in the manner of a pick'. The same author also informs us that it 'is the universal and, I believe, the only agricultural implement in use in West Africa'. Despite its somewhat prosaic function, the hoe is not without a religious or magical aspect. In Nigeria, according to P. A. Talbot,[2] 'medicine' is poured on the hoes as a protection against theft; so that 'when a thief enters a farm which is protected in this way, one of them springs into his hand, and he is forced to hoe and hoe until the owner arrives and releases him'.

A peculiarity of this type of hoe is the very acute angle of the handle, in conjunction with a very large blade,[3] and its superiority in manufacture compared with those from other parts of West Africa. The artistic faculties of the Mandingos, a race said to have founded the great empire of Ghana in A.D. 320,[4] are confined to the making of objects of craft and industry,[5] a limitation urged, if not imposed, by their Mohammedan religion.

The place Kombo, whence the hoe is said to have been collected, is probably the same village of 'Koomboo' visited by Mungo Park in 1795[6] during the last stages of his great journey. Its inhabitants had such a bad reputation that he felt compelled to spend the night in the fields, despite 'there being great appearance of rain'.

Door screen (left background in photograph).
    Cane; L. 69"; W. 40¼", 39".
    Stated to be 'from Logone Birrimi, Kotoko tribe, Northern Cameroons'.
    British Museum. (Collected by Miss O. Macleod, 1911.)

The canes are of very thin bamboo, held together by fibre binding, dyed purplish pink and dark brown (sepia), the latter possibly faded from black. The binding is arranged in a curvilinear pattern forming three vertical bands. The former colour is probably obtained by mixing the two dyes, said to be made in this region,[7] namely indigo, and red obtained from an acacia.

The dwellings of the Kotoko tribe, on the Logone River, whence Miss Macleod collected this specimen, are described by her[7] as two-storied Mohammedan houses. The purpose of the door-screen was probably to allow the air and strong light to

[1] *Travels and Life in Ashanti and Jaman,* 1898, p. 418.

[2] P. A. Talbot, *Southern Nigeria,* vol. ii.

[3] Cf. similar one in the British Museum, from McCarthy Island Province, Gambia.

[4] Op. cit., vol. i.

[5] Mungo Park, *Travels in the Interior of Africa,* Everyman ed., p. 215.

[6] Op. cit., p. 269.

[7] Olive Macleod, *Chiefs and Cities of Central Africa, across Lake Chad,* London, 1912, p. 120.

filter in while preventing the Mohammedan female occupants from being seen from outside.

Section of wattle fence or crinting, used in house construction (right background in photograph).

> Split bamboo; H. 42"; W. 38".
> Stated to be 'from Gambia'.
> Probably Mandingo tribe.
> *British Museum.* (Formerly in the Imperial Institute.)

This section of fence is shown in the photograph placed on its side. It is made of strips of bamboo cane ($\frac{7}{8}$" wide); three of which placed together form each upright, across which other strips of cane are interlaced.

This type of fence is used in the construction of Mandingo dwellings; such were observed in the region of the River Gambia as far back as 1795 by Mungo Park,[1] who describes them as follows: 'All the huts belonging to the same family are surrounded by a fence, constructed of bamboo canes split and formed into a sort of wicker-work. The whole enclosure is called a *sirk* or *surk*. A number of these enclosures, with narrow passages between them, form what is called a town; but the huts are generally placed without any regularity, according to the caprice of the owner.'

PLATE XXXI

GOLD WEIGHTS, SPOON FOR LIFTING GOLD DUST, BOX FOR STORING GOLD DUST, FINGER RINGS

Gold weight (*mrammuo*) representing a chief carried in a litter on the heads of two bearers, with a figure behind carrying a bag and an animal on his back (top left in photograph).

> Brass casting; H. $3\frac{5}{8}$".
> Ashanti tribe, Gold Coast.
> *Curtis Moffat Collection.*

This specimen and the others illustrated in this plate are, excepting the spoon, cast by the process known as 'cire-perdue'; the subject is modelled in wax together with a 'moulding stick' and the whole placed in a clay cover so that when heated the wax pours out through the channel formed by the moulding stick and the molten metal can be poured in instead.[2] The weights are used in the market for measuring gold dust, each design meaning a definite degree. This weight is a very large one.

---

[1] Everyman ed., p. 15.   [2] R. S. Rattray, *Ashanti*. ch. xxv.

The circular back of the litter is ornamented with a design resembling a web, and the under surface is also decorated with a pattern.

T. E. Bowdich[1] describes the caboceers or captains borne in hammocks at his reception at Coomassie. 'The state hammocks, like long cradles, were raised in the rear, the poles on the heads of the bearers; the cushions and pillows were covered with crimson taffeta, and the richest cloths hung over the sides.'

Hammock men, according to Rattray,[2] were in charge of the King's sheep, pigs, and fowls, as well as having the duty of preparing the King's bath.

Gold weight representing a mounted person wearing a circular cap (top centre).
> Brass casting; H. $4\frac{1}{4}$".
> Ashanti tribe, Gold Coast.
> *Curtis Moffat Collection.*

This specimen is an exceptionally large weight, cast in solid metal.

Gold weight representing an elephant (left in photograph).
> Brass casting; H. $1\frac{1}{4}$"; L. 4".
> Ashanti.
> *Curtis Moffat Collection.*

The colour of the metal is bright yellow and lighter than is the case with the other specimens illustrated.

Gold weight representing a river fish, sometimes known as mud-fish or shad-fish (centre in photograph).
> Brass casting; L. (side of head to tail) $2\frac{1}{8}$"; L. (front of head to body) $1\frac{7}{8}$".
> Ashanti.
> *Curtis Moffat Collection.*

The colour of the metal is that of dark bronze and it is cast hollow inside.

Gold weight representing a drummer beating two talking drums *ntumpane* (left).
> Brass casting; H. $2\frac{1}{4}$"; W. $1\frac{3}{4}$"; D. 1".
> Ashanti.
> *Oxford, Pitt-Rivers Museum*, 1926.

The figure of the man is depicted wearing a loin-cloth, and with horizontal incisions across the front of the body and neck. The hair is in the form of spiral coils resembling that of a gold weight illustrated by Rattray,[3] according to whom, this mode

[1] *Mission to Ashantee*, 1817, London ed., 1873, p. 34.

[2] *Religion and Art in Ashanti*, p. 134.

[3] *Ashanti*, Fig. 125, and p. 309.

of dressing the hair is 'called *mpese*, formerly adopted by executioners, now only by the priests'. The small projection on the shoulders is the unfiled end of the 'moulding stick' which is left thus to make the weight correct.[1]

The two drums are similar, each with small circular base and pegs for stretching the membrane. They represent the large type of Ashanti drum which is employed in a pair and is used to sound long-distance messages by combining the high note of one drum with the low note of the other, to indicate the tonal sounds of speech;[2] the pair of supports and drum sticks are always made of a special kind of wood. The 'eyes' of the drums are not indicated, unless the diagonal grooves on the side are intended for them.

There is an Ashanti proverb[3] which this gold weight perhaps illustrates: 'No one takes his talking drums and goes and beats them in the war camp to which he has fled.'

Gold weight representing a leopard with his front paws on the back of a tortoise (right in photograph).

Brass casting; H. $1\frac{7}{8}''$; L. $2\frac{7}{8}''$; W. $\frac{3}{4}''$.

Ashanti.

Edgar Ainsworth Collection.

The subject of the leopard with its prey, in the form of various smaller creatures, is frequently employed as a gold weight motif.

The tortoise is depicted stretching its head forward and vainly trying to raise one of its front legs in order to remove the obstruction.

There are two Ashanti proverbs,[4] of which either may be the subject of this specimen: 'When a leopard catches a tortoise, it turns it over and over in vain'; 'The leopard declares he prowls the bush to no purpose, and that the tortoise really owns his jungle kingdom.' Rattray informs us that the latter saying is based on the following story: 'A leopard was prowling about the bush in search of prey, and suddenly seeing a tortoise, sprang on it, exclaiming *"Manyâ Wo,"* "I've got you." The tortoise, however, replied, "As for you I have been watching you long before you ever saw me." The saying is quoted in the sense that, a king may think he knows all about the affairs of his subjects; whereas in reality they probably know a great deal more about his.'

Gold weight representing two old men meeting (bottom right in photograph).

Brass casting; H. $1\frac{1}{2}''$; D. $1\frac{1}{8}''$; W. $1\frac{1}{8}''$.

Ashanti.

Edgar Ainsworth Collection.

[1] Op. cit., p. 308.   [2] Op. cit., ch. xxii.   [4] R. S. Rattray, *Ashanti Proverbs*, Oxford,
[3] Op. cit., p. 309.   1916, p. 62.

Each figure is depicted leaning backwards, with his left arm bent round to touch his chin. It represents a subject frequently employed for gold weights and is described by Rattray[1] as follows: 'The meeting of the famous old men known throughout Ashanti as Amoaka and Adu, two legendary friends who met again after many years of separation, both having encountered misfortune and become very poor. In many castings one of them is depicted carrying a bunch of keys, all he has left to show of former wealth.'

Gold weight representing a fly-whisk (bottom left in photograph).

    Brass casting; H. $3\frac{1}{2}''$; W. $1''$.

    Ashanti.

    Oxford, Pitt-Rivers Museum, 1930.

The type of fly-whisk which this gold weight represents is formed from an elephant's tail. Dr. R. Zeller[2] illustrates four different examples of this subject, and states that 'elephant tails are emblems of chief's rank', being 'the insignia of second and third-rate chiefs.'

Spoon (*nsawa*) for lifting gold dust and putting it in the scales.

    Beaten brass, L. $4\frac{1}{8}''$; W. $1\frac{1}{4}''$.

    Ashanti.

    Curtis Moffat Collection.

The spoon is made in very thin brass and the pattern is beaten in relief.[3]

Box (*mmumpuruwa*) for storing gold dust.

    Brass casting; L. $2\frac{3}{4}''$; W. $1\frac{1}{2}''$; H. $1\frac{3}{4}''$.

    Ashanti.

    Curtis Moffat Collection.

The box is cast in two separate pieces, namely box and lid. The latter fits inside the former without the use of a hinge. The colour is dark bronze. The lid is ornamented with two heads of human beings. Besides being used for storing gold dust, such boxes are also used sometimes as weights and are also said to be given by chiefs as presents filled with gold.

Finger-ring with a figure of a man riding on a horse, and supporting a pan on his head, said to be used for snuff (top right in photograph).

    Brass casting; H. $4\frac{1}{2}''$.

    Probably Ashanti.

    Curtis Moffat Collection.

[1] *Ashanti*, p. 312.
[2] *Die Goldgewichte von Asante*, Pl. x.
[3] Similar spoons illustrated by Rattray, *Ashanti*, Fig. 113, also Zeller, op. cit., Pl. i.

Finger-ring with a figure of a bird, probably the Ibis, with outstretched wings supporting a pan, said to be used for snuff (right in photograph).
>   Brass casting; H. 4½".
>   Probably Ashanti.
>   *Curtis Moffat Collection.*

White woven cloth with blue striped border.
>   Cotton; L. 47"; W. 14½".
>   Stated to be 'from Abeokuta', Yoruba tribe, Nigeria.
>   *Halifax, Bankfield Museum.*
This cloth was woven on the 'continuous warp' loom, using two colours only.

PLATE XXXII
WINE-VESSEL, LAMP, TOBACCO-BOX, AND PIPES

Wine vessel in the form of a woman's head.
>   Earthenware; H. 10¼"; Diam. 5½".
>   Stated to be 'from Buri (Diri?) Bomokandi River, Mangbettu tribe, Northern
>   Belgian Congo'.
>   *British Museum*, 1921.

This vessel is said to be used for containing banana wine (*poma*) which is drunk by the elders in connexion with boys' initiation ceremonies.

The earthenware is thick and coarse, and is dark grey in colour. The patterns are sunk or incised, and are said to be obtained by impressing string. Unlike the custom in most parts of Africa, the manufacture of this pottery is said to be exclusively the work of men.[1]

The upper part of the vessel represents the head of a Mangbettu woman, the raised eyebrows and high, narrow head being characteristic features of Mangbettu women due to their custom, according to Dr. H. Schubotz[2] 'of lengthening the skull by means of a bandage firmly wound round the head of an infant from the forehead upwards. As the head develops, this bandage is loosened from time to time, and the result is that the top of the skull acquires a conical shape. . . . It certainly improves the physiognomy by raising the upper eye-lids, so that the Mangbettu women appear to possess larger eyes than other negresses.' The band of pattern on the cheeks probably depicts the skin decoration, which the same author calls tattooing, practised only by the women.[3]

[1] *From the Congo to the Nile* (Duke of Mecklenburg), vol. ii, p. 54, also Fig. 36.
[2] Op. cit., pp. 50, 51.
[3] Op. cit., p. 50.

The mouth of the vessel is formed to exploit the curious shape of the Mangbettu woman's coiffure, to make which, we are informed,[1] 'they twist their hair into numerous thin plaits which are arranged on a thin wooden erection resembling an oyster-basket. This hair-dressing naturally occupies a great many hours, and is consequently worn for several weeks at a time.'

This people are, in the opinion of the same author,[2] noted for their intelligence, beauty, skill, and good taste, by which 'they have attained in the Congo basin a position similar to that held by the French in Europe during the seventeenth century'.

Tobacco-box in the form of a bird, with tail forming the stopper.

> Hard wood; L. 6½.
> Stated to have been 'presented by the King of Kiama for services rendered'.
> Probably Borgo tribe, NW. Nigeria.
> *British Museum.*

The box consists of two pieces of which the colour is brownish-black. The cord tied round the neck of the bird is woven from pink and green coloured cotton. The tail is formed with a peg which fits like a stopper into the box; and the latter contains some powdery tobacco, said to be very aromatic and usually chewed.

Lamp (suspended near the top of the photograph).

> Earthenware; H. 6¾".
> Stated to be 'from Paga, Kassena or Nankanni (Frafra) tribes, Northern Territories, Gold Coast'.
> *British Museum*, 1922. (Collected by A. W. Cardinall.)

The vessel is moulded in black pottery. It is perforated with a number of openings in the bowl, and has a looped handle at the top by which it may be suspended.

The lamp is one of a pair which Mr. Cardinall bought in the open market at Paga, where they were 'offered at 300 cowries apiece by a Nankanni girl'.[3] This specimen is described by him as a 'slush lamp, such as the Talansi, Nankanni, Kassena, and Builsa tribes of the Northern Territories use to light their huts'; the wick consists 'merely of a piece of old cloth floating on shea-butter'.

---

[1] Op. cit., p. 51. [2] Op. cit., p. 43.
[3] A. W. Cardinall, 'Fire and Fire-making', *Man*, Sept. 1923, p. 85.

Pipe with a long stem and a bowl in the form of an elephant's head (right in photograph).

> Brass, wood, beads; H. 22½; W. 2¼; D. 4¼.
> Stated to be 'from Bagam, Cameroons'.
> Probably Bamoum tribe.
> *Cambridge University Museum*, 1921. (Collected by Captain L. W. G. Malcolm.)

This pipe is described as a 'Head-chief's insignia of office'.[1] It consists of three separate pieces, namely a bowl, with socket, of brass, the long stem of wood covered with beads, and mouthpiece of brass. The bowl consists of a socket in which the wooden stem is inserted, joined to a loop in the form of an elephant's head with its trunk curled underneath and with two pairs of tusks. The wooden stem is covered with cloth, to which is sewn the covering of glass trade beads, of which the colours are dark blue (ultramarine) (dark tone in the photograph) arranged in zigzag bands alternately with pale pink (light tone) in the centre section and with pale blue (same light tone as the pink in the photograph) in the remainder. The mouthpiece consists of a plain brass tube, ¼″ diameter (not visible in the photograph), the end of which is inserted in the top of the stem.

The pipe exemplifies the work of two crafts in which the Bamoum specialize, namely bead-work coverings and brass-casting. The representation of the elephant's head is a favourite device in Bamoum art not only in brass castings,[2] but also for dance masks[3] made of wood and painted.

Water-pipe (centre in photograph).

> Gourd, copper, earthenware; L. (gourd) 16″; W. (gourd) 4″.
> Stated to be 'from Awemba tribe, Northern Rhodesia'.
> *British Museum*, 1909.

The stem and the bowl for containing the water are formed from a gourd artificially shaped. The smoke is drawn from the pottery pipe bowl, through the water, in the manner of the Arab *narghileh*, from which it may be derived.

The gourd is deep orange in colour, and is decorated with pieces of copper-wire stitched to it. The pipe bowl is moulded in black pottery, and is decorated with an

[1] Capt. L. W. G. Malcolm, 'Brass-casting in the Central Cameroons,' *Man*, Jan. 1923, and illustrated (with a different stem), Pl. A, No. 2, Fig. 2.

[2] Cf. similar example from Bagam, in Liverpool Museum; and examples 'from Bamum' illustrated F. W. H. Migeod, *Through British Cameroons*, p. 123, and E. von Sydow, *Die Kunst der Naturvölker*, p. 125.

[3] Cf. example in Liverpool Museum.

incised pattern. The stem over which it is placed consists of a piece of cane fitted inside a collar made of gourd; this stem is inserted into a hole cut in the gourd bowl and is bound with sinew cord.

The gourd form and decoration is characteristic of a craft practised among the Awemba[1] and surrounding tribes; copper being much employed in the region of Lake Tanganyika.

G. R. Carline states, regarding a series obtained by him[2] from the village of Chief Pande: 'Women seemed to be the principal smokers; a woman, whom I watched pounding grain, took frequent rests for the purpose of a smoke; she kept the pottery bowl in the folds of her dress, while the gourd stem which contained the water was left lying about on the ground.'

Fan (partly shown at the top of the photograph).

> Skin; Diam. 14".
> Stated to be 'from Benin' (Bini tribe), Southern Nigeria.
> *Captain A. W. F. Fuller Collection.* (Collected by Ralph Locke.)

The fan consists of a circular piece of thick cow's hide covered with black hair, and a wooden handle, 10" long (not visible in the Plate), which is also covered with the hide. The designs represent an elephant (upside down in the photograph), an animal venerated among the Bini, and on either side two hair combs (only the handles visible), of the large wooden type made by the Jekri. The central design (partly visible) probably represents a stylized human figure. The designs give to the black glossy surface of the fan a rich effect in colour, being of bright red flannel stitched with a border of thin yellow skin.

The fan is an example of the type usually made by the Bini and Jekri tribes, and is probably from the former, as it is said to have been collected at Benin; Ralph Locke, the collector, being one of the two survivors of the famous massacre which followed Consul Phillips's attempt to visit Benin in 1897 against the King's wishes.

One of the bronze plaques collected by the subsequent punitive expedition to Benin, and now in the British Museum, shows two naked youths holding fans of this type. These persons, whose duty it was to fan the King, were called *ukoba*, King's boys.[3] They wore no clothes, barring the fan, until they were married, and were also the King's agents and executioners.

---

[1] Very similar specimen in Batley Museum.

[2] In Bankfield Museum, Halifax.

[3] Cyril Punch, quoted by H. Ling Roth, *Great Benin*, p. 123.

PLATE I

THE RECEPTION
Painted wood
Lagos, Nigeria (Egba-Yoruba tribe)

PLATE II

THE DRUMMER AND ANOTHER FIGURE
Painted wood
Loango, Belgian Congo (Bavili (?) tribe)

PLATE III

THE LISTENER
(*another view of seated figure in Plate II*)
Painted wood
Loango, Belgian Congo (Bavili (?) tribe)

PLATE IV

GODDESS AND CHILD
Painted wood
Lagos, Nigeria (Egba-Yoruba tribe)

PLATE V

GODDESS AND CHILD (*another view*)
Painted wood
Lagos, Nigeria (Egba-Yoruba tribe)

PLATE VI

BEARDED MAN
Wood
Ivory Coast (Baoule (?) tribe)

PLATE VII

WOMAN WITH BOWL
(another view of figure in Plate IX)
Wood
Belgian Congo (Ba-Luba tribe)

PLATE VIII

MOTHER SEATED WITH CHILDREN
Wood
Northern Nigeria (Yoruba tribe)

PLATE IX

ANCESTOR FIGURE AND TWO OTHERS
WITH OFFERING BOWLS

Centre: Copper-sheeted wood. Gabun (Bakota (?) tribe)
Right: Painted wood. N. Nigeria (Yoruba tribe)
Left: Blackened wood. Belgian Congo (Ba-Luba tribe)

PLATE X

WOMAN SUPPORTING STOOL
Wood
Belgian Congo (Maniema tribe)

PLATE XI

A WHITE MAN VISITS A CHIEF

Door in painted wood

Nigeria (Yoruba tribe)

PLATE XII

A CHIEF WITH HIS WIVES

Red earthenware

Gold Coast (Fanti (?) tribe)

PLATE XIII

THREE-FACED MASK
Skin-covered wood, painted, with metal eyes
Cross River, Cameroon (Ekoi (?) tribe)

PLATE XIV

APRONED WOMAN; MAN IN CAP; MAN WITH DRESSED HAIR
Wood
Left: Sierra Leone (Mendi tribe)
Centre and right: Gabun (?)
Copyright Wellcome Historical Medical Museum

PLATE XV

WOMAN'S HEAD
Mask in blackened wood
Ivory Coast (Baoule (?) tribe)

PLATE XVI

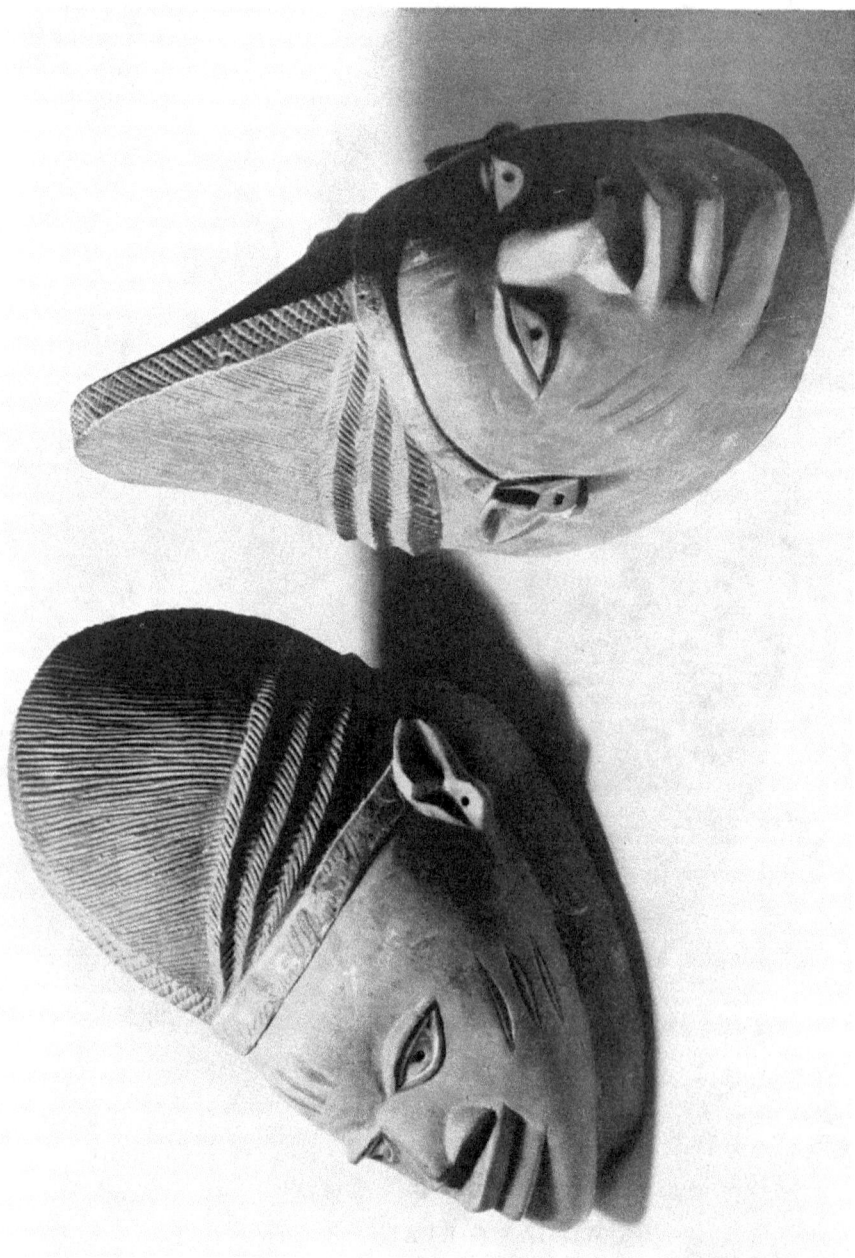

WOMEN ANCESTORS

Masks in painted wood. Lagos, Nigeria (Egba-Yoruba tribe)

PLATE XVII

CRESTED HEAD AND TWO-FACED HORNED HEAD
Skin-covered wood with metal eyes
Cross River, Nigeria (Ekoi (?) tribe)
Copyright Wellcome Historical Medical Museum

PLATE XVIII

INITIATION MASK WITH PLAITED HAIR
Painted wood
Belgian Congo (Ba-Pende tribe)

PLATE XIX

GHOST MASK OF WOMAN
Painted wood
Gabun (Ashira (?) tribe)

PLATE XX

WHITE MASK WITH SCARLET EYES
Painted wood
S. Nigeria (Ibo (?) tribe)

PLATE XXI

WHITE MASK WITH SCARLET EYES (*another view*)
Painted wood
S. Nigeria (Ibo (?) tribe)

PLATE XXII

WATER POT

Black glazed earthenware. Gold Coast (Ashanti tribe)

PLATE XXIII

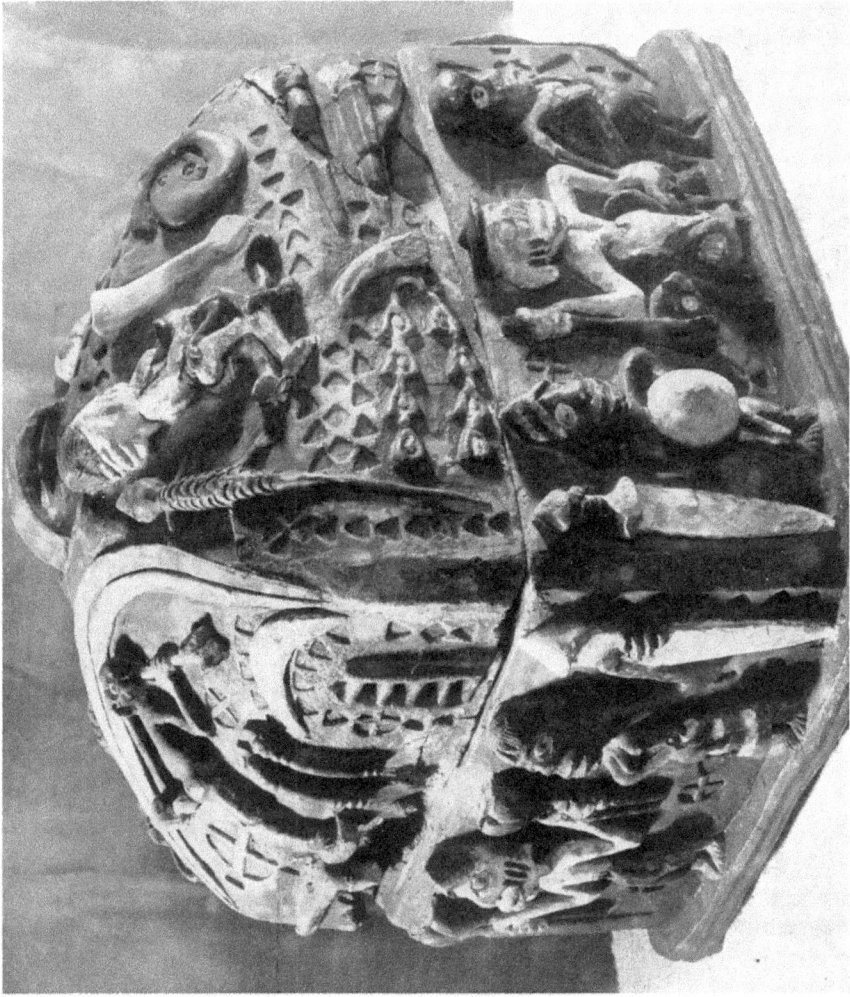

LIDDED VESSEL.
Painted earthenware. Dahomey

PLATE XXIV

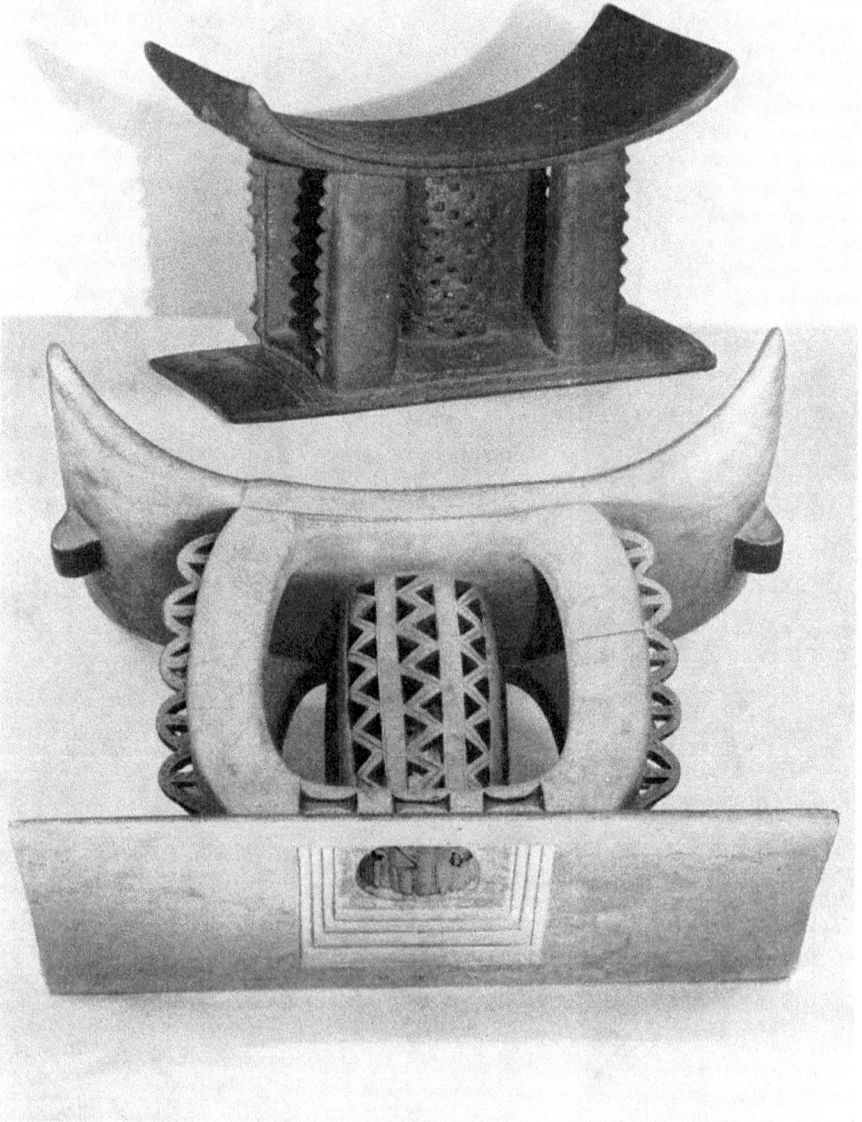

TWO STOOLS
Light wood; blackened wood
Gold Coast (Ashanti tribe)

PLATE XXV

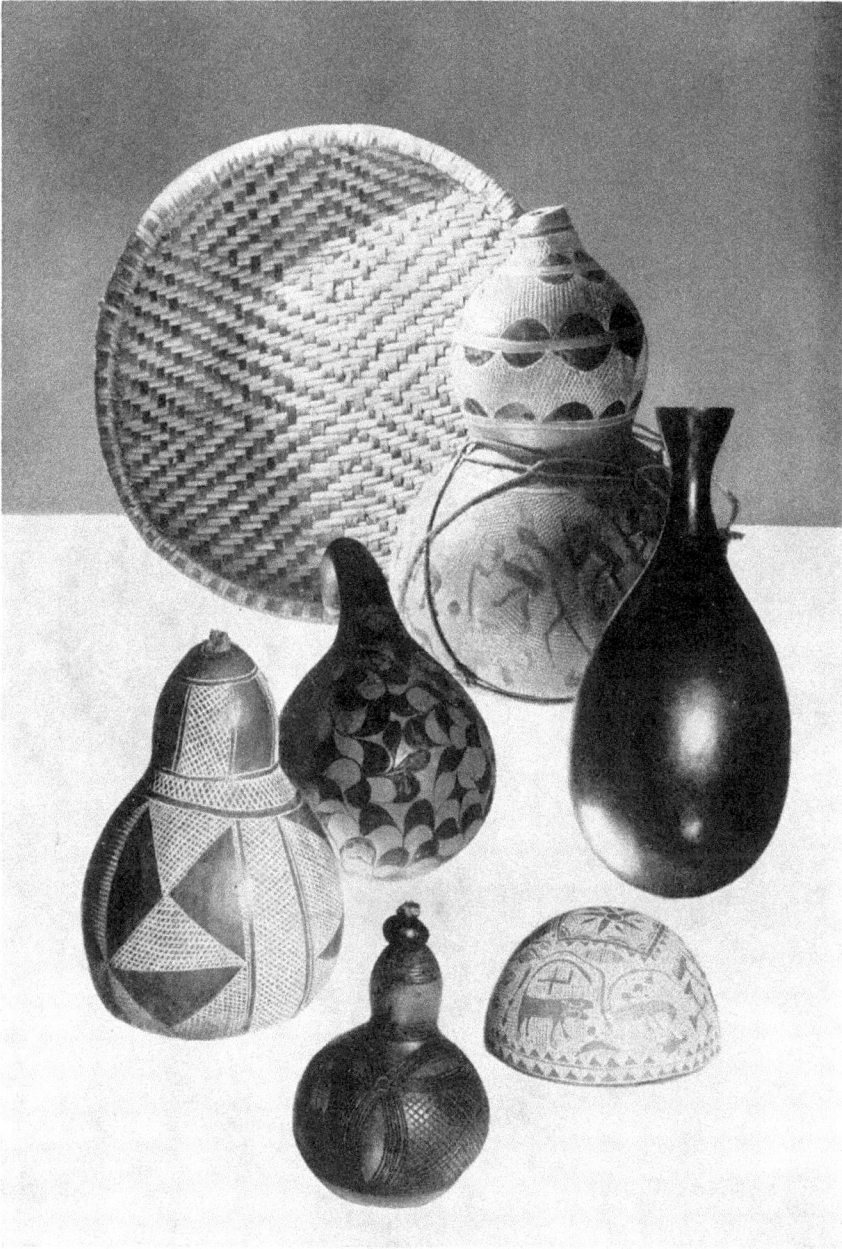

GOURDS AND BASKET TRAY

Gourds: *top*, Angola (Kongo (?) tribe); *right*, Fernando Po (Bubi tribe); *centre*, Nigeria (Efik (?) tribe); *left*, Sierra Leone (Mendi tribe); *bottom right*, Gold Coast (Fanti (?) tribe); *bottom*, S. Africa (?)

Basket: Angola (Bihe tribe)

PLATE XXVI

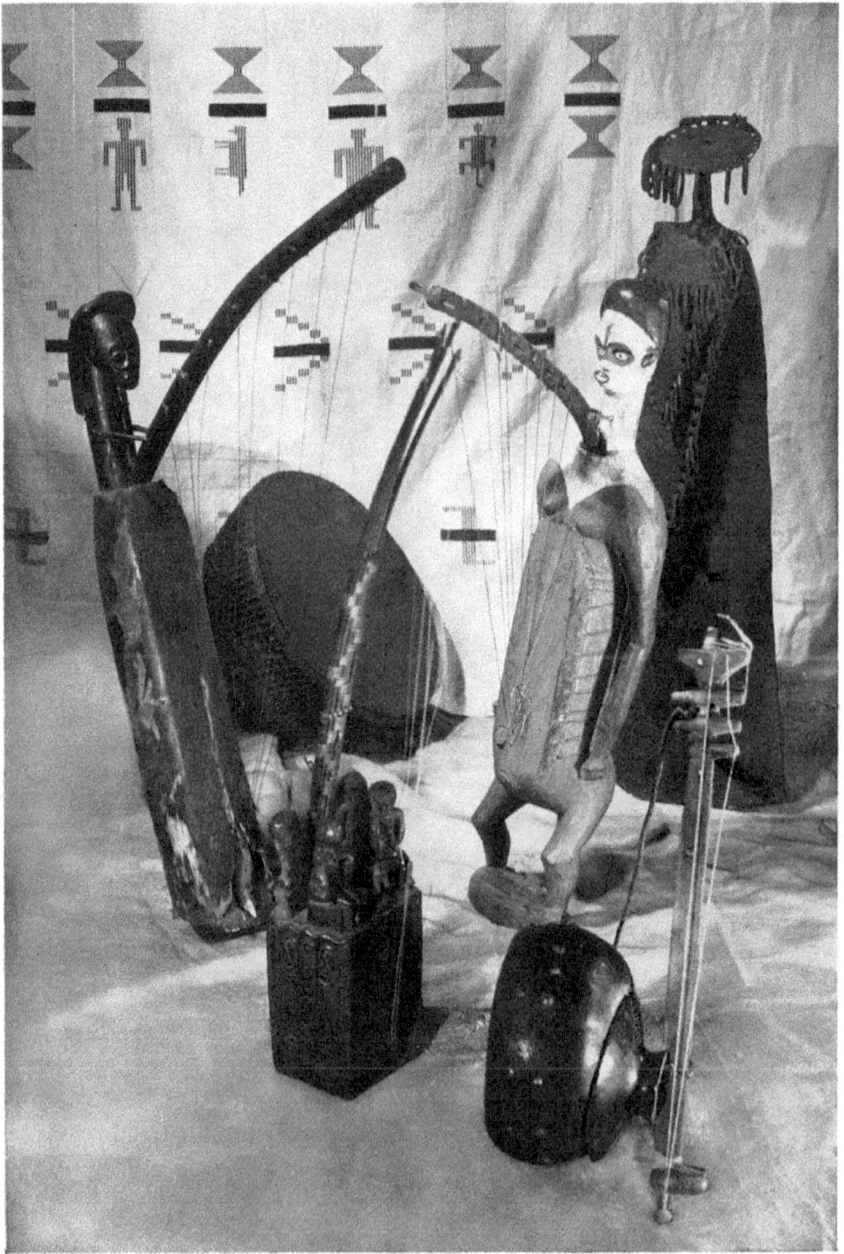

MUSICAL INSTRUMENTS

Harps: *right centre*, Gabun (Commi (?) tribe); *left*, Gabun (Bakalai (?) tribe)
Harp-guitar: *centre foreground*, Gabun (Chekiani (?) tribe)
Fiddle: *foreground*, Belgian Congo (Basonge tribe)
Gong: *right*, N. Nigeria (Guari tribe). Drum: *background*, S. Nigeria (?)

PLATE XXVII

HARPS
(another view, see Plate XXVI)
Left, Gabun (Commi (?) tribe); *right*, Gabun (Bakalai (?) tribe)

PLATE XXVIII

HEAD OF HARP-GUITAR
(another view, see Plate XXVI)
Gabun (Chekiani (?) tribe)

PLATE XXIX

CEREMONIAL HOE, HEAD-RESTS, AND RITUAL BOWL

Hoe: *top right*, Belgian Congo (Ba-Kongo tribe)

Head-rests: *left foreground*, Belgian Congo (N. Ba-Mbala tribe); *right foreground*, Angola (Zombo tribe)

Bowl: *top left*, Dahomey

PLATE XXX

CANOE PADDLES AND HOE

Ceremonial paddle: *centre*, S. Nigeria (Kalabari tribe)

Paddles: *left*, S. Nigeria (Jekri tribe); *foreground*, S. Nigeria (Sobo tribe); *right*, Angola (Mussorongo(?) tribe)

Hoe: *centre*, Gambia (Mandingo tribe)

PLATE XXXI

GOLD WEIGHTS, SPOON, BOX, AND RINGS
Brass
Gold Coast (Ashanti tribe)

PLATE XXXII

WINE VESSEL, LAMP, TOBACCO BOX, AND PIPES

Vessel: *left*, N. Belgian Congo (Mangbettu tribe)
Lamp: *top right*, Northern Territories, Gold Coast (Fra-fra tribe)
Box: *right foreground*, N. Nigeria (Borgo tribe)
Pipes: *centre*, Northern Rhodesia (Awemba tribe); *right*, Cameroon (Bamoum tribe)

BIBLIOGRAPHY RELATING TO INDIGENOUS ART IN TROPICAL AFRICA

I. *General* (*Sculpture, Weaving, Pottery, Bronzes, &c.*)

1. PORTIER, A., and PONCETTON, F. LES ARTS SAUVAGES, AFRIQUE. (Libraire Albert Morancé, Paris, 1930.) 250 francs.

The 50 plates (a few in colour) are among the best of reproductions. The works illustrated come from French Guinea, Gabun, French Portuguese and Belgian Congo, Ivory Coast, Nigeria, Senegal, Dahomey. They are drawn from French collections.

2. FROBENIUS, LEO, and BREUIL, HENRI. L'AFRIQUE. (*Cahiers d'art*, Nos. 8–9, Paris, 1930.) 30 francs.

First-rate illustrations, especially of Bushman art and of Nigerian sculpture. The long article by Frobenius is romantic and gives an idealized picture of earlier African cultures. The illustrations are valuable. A considerable part of the book is devoted to prehistoric weapons.

3. HAUSENSTEIN, WILHELM. BARBAREN UND KLASSIKER. (Munich, Piper & Co., 1923.) R.marks 15.

169 excellent illustrations. A comparative study, including Polynesia, Western Tropical Africa, Brazil, North America, Mexico, Peru, Ecuador, Sumatra, Borneo, India, Bali, Burma, Cambodia, Java, China, Japan, Persia.
Good for comparative illustration.

4. KÜHN, HERBERT. DIE KUNST DER PRIMITIVEN. (Munich, Delphin Verlag, 1920.) Cloth, R.marks 30; half cloth, R.marks 38.

This well-illustrated book gives a short account of Palaeolithic Art including the drawings of Bushmen and the pictures at Altamira in North Spain. It gives a short account of the rock pictures in North-Western America and of the Neolithic and Bronze Ages in Europe. Chapter IX is on the Art of Negro Africa (Cameroons, Urua, Congo, Yoruba); Chapter XIII on the Art of Benin.

5. SYDOW, ECKART VON. DIE KUNST DER NATURVÖLKER UND DER VORZEIT, Vol. I, PROPYLÄENKUNSTGESCHICHTE. (Berlin, Propyläen Verlag, 1923.) Half cloth, R.marks 45; half leather, R.marks 50.

This book, which has 490 excellent illustrations (some in colour) and a good short bibliography, is an introduction to the art of primitive peoples, including Africa, Polynesia, and Australia, Indonesia, the North-American Indians, Mexico, ancient South American cultures and European pre-history.
It is the best general introduction to the whole subject.

BIBLIOGRAPHY

6. WITHERS GILL, J. HANDBOOK AND GUIDE TO THE AFRICAN COLLEC-
TION IN THE PUBLIC MUSEUMS, LIVERPOOL. 1931. 6*d*.

A brief description of an important collection of examples of African art and handicraft
in the Liverpool Museums. In a short introduction Mr. Withers Gill touches on the connexion between indigenous art and religion. The handbook has eleven plates and a map.

7. TOGO-CAMEROUN. A monthly magazine published (27 Bd. des Italiens, Paris) by
L'Agence économique des territoires africains sous mandat. 12 fr. per number.

The issue for February, 1931, which contains an introductory article by Professor
Labouret of the École coloniale and École nationale des langues orientales vivantes, is
devoted to the Bamiléké people and has good illustrations of their houses, tattoo marks,
pottery and textiles.

8. FROBENIUS, LEO. DAS STERBENDE AFRIKA, Vol. I. Quarto, pp. xi+86, with
30 lithographic illustrations (some in colour) and 57 woodcuts. (München: O. C.
Recht Verlag.) 12*s*.

Full of first-hand and sympathetic observation of African life and custom. Written with
romantic emotion. The illustrations cover nearly all forms of design and decorative pattern,
drawn from Northern, Subequatorial, and Western Equatorial Africa.

9. SYDOW, ECKART VON. EXOTISCHE KUNST, AFRIKA UND OZEANIEN.
(Leipzig: Klinkhardt and Biermann, 1921.) R.marks 2.

A cheap book with 41 plates, some good. It has a fairly good introduction, drawing
distinctions between African and Polynesian art and emphasizing the connexion between
African sculpture and some sides of modern art.

10. NEGRO ANTHOLOGY, made by NANCY CUNARD, 1931–3. Published by Nancy
Cunard at Wishart & Co., 9, John Street, London, W. 2. Quarto (12″ × 8½″), pp.
viii+855. £2 2*s*.

This book, 'an anthology of some 150 voices of both races', records 'the struggles and
achievements, the persecutions and the revolts against them, of the Negro peoples'. It is a
unique and striking miscellany, with contributions from the United States, West Indies, and
South America, Europe, and Africa. A group of essays deals with music in America, Africa,
and the West Indies. The book contains 84 plates of West African sculpture, and papers
on this and related subjects by Ladislas Szecsi, Charles Ratton, Henri Lavachery, Raymond
Michelet, and others.

II. *Sculpture*

11. EINSTEIN, CARL. AFRIKANISCHE PLASTIK, Vol. VII. ORBIS PICTUS.
(Berlin: Wasmuth, 1925.) R.marks 3.

A cheap book with 48 good plates. The works are assigned to their respective regions.
The best are of the Yoruba, Benin, Cameroons, French Congo, Urua, and Bakongo.
The illustrations are taken from museums in Germany and Belgium.

BIBLIOGRAPHY

12. Einstein, Carl. NEGERPLASTIK. (Munich: Kurt Wolff, 1920.) Half cloth, R.marks 10; half leather, R.marks 14.

116 good illustrations. The introduction emphasizes the connexion between African Art and Religion and the cubistic character of much of the sculpture.

13. Guillaume, Paul, and Munro, Thomas. PRIMITIVE NEGRO SCULPTURE. (Jonathan Cape, 1926.) 25s.

This is the most systematic account of negro sculpture which has been published in English. Its 41 illustrations are taken from the Collection of the Barnes Foundation at Merion, Pennsylvania.

It gives an account of the growth of interest in African art with brief references to anthropological journals. There is a short reference to African music. It gives an historical account, so far as this is possible, of the origins of sculpture in West Central Africa, and its conjectural relations to Egyptian, Hindu, and Chinese art. It defines the area from which the most important art works come, viz. Ivory Coast and Gabun, the south-western Sudan, the Upper and Lower Congo, French Guinea, Dahomey, Benin, and Cameroons. It specifies the tribes which have been specially prominent in the production of art, viz. the Baule, Bobo, Agui, Mossi, Gouro, and Dan; the M'Fang and M'Pongwe in the Gabun region, and, farther south and east, the Bushongo, Baluba, Sibiti, Sangha, Bambalu, Bakelele, Gwembi, Yungu, and Bangongo.

The book reviews the different types of art-work produced by Western Tropical Africa—singing, symbolic dancing, story telling, pottery making, weaving of palmcloth, plaiting, tattooing, decoration of musical instruments, the making of masks and fetishes of hard wood and occasionally of metals, ivory, horn, stone, or plaster.

The book ends with a chapter on the relation of African sculpture to contemporary art.

14. Maes, J., and Lavachery, H. ART NÈGRE. (Libraire nationale d'art et d'histoire, Brussels and Paris, 1930.) 6s.

48 plates of illustrations. The first-named author is Conservateur de la section ethnographique du Musée du Congo at Tervueren, Belgium. The illustrations are confined to sculpture, most of the pieces being in the Musée du Congo, with reinforcements from French and German collections. The examples include two or three minor masterpieces and an interesting piece of modern work. The introduction by Dr. Maes, entitled 'La Sculpture au Congo belge' is scholarly, discriminating, and temperate, with valuable sidelights on technique and social tradition. The bearing of indigenous habits of child-training on the power of direct observation is discussed. The writers' conclusion is that the deep source of artistic power in the tribes of the Belgian Congo lies in the social and religious tradition of the indigenous family and tribe.

15. Sydow, Eckart von. HANDBUCH DER WESTAFRIKANISCHEN PLASTIK. Vol. I, DIE WESTAFRIKANISCHE PLASTIK. (Berlin: Reimer and Vohsen, 1930.) R.marks 40.

10 illustrations. The most systematic account of West African sculpture. It deals in detail with Senegambia, Sierra Leone, Liberia, Ivory Coast, Gold Coast, South Togo,

Southern Nigeria, Cameroons, French Equatorial Africa, the Lower Congo, South Belgian Congo, and Northern Angola. Examples are mostly taken from the Berlin and Leipzig Museums, but also from the British Museum and from Paris.

III. *Bronzes*

16. LUSCHAN, F. VON. DIE ALTERTÜMER VON BENIN. (Berlin, Walter de Gruyter & Co., 1919.) 3 volumes, R.marks 150.

17. GEORGES HARDY. L'ART NÈGRE, L'ART ANIMISTE DES NOIRS D'AFRIQUE. (Paris: Henri Laurens, 1927.) Small 4to, pp. 168. Fr. 18.

This excellent and thoughtful book, by the Director of the École coloniale, is one of a series on Art and Religion. It is illustrated by twenty-four well-chosen examples drawn from the Ivory Coast, Belgian Congo, Loango, Dahomey, Sudan, Cameroons, Gabun, and Benin. There is a condensed bibliography. The author surveys the influence of animism, of the worship of the dead and of spirits, and of the habits of secret societies on artistic creation. He discusses the effect which the forces of nature, racial experience, and the strictness of tribal discipline have had on negro art. In a final chapter (with the hesitations and provisos which reveal his great knowledge of the subject) he sketches the regional divisions of West African Art, its present decadence, the causes of its decline, and the hope of a revival when the mental equilibrium, shaken by waves of European influence, shall have been restored.

18. READ, C. HERCULES, and DALTON, O. M. ANTIQUITIES FROM THE CITY OF BENIN AND FROM OTHER PARTS OF WEST AFRICA IN THE BRITISH MUSEUM. (Trustees of the British Museum, 1899.) Half cloth, 25*s*.; half morocco, 34*s*.

32 full-page plates, with other illustrations in text. A scholarly and sumptuous volume, with excellent historical introduction and chapters on Ivory, European influence, Dress, Ornaments, and Weapons, and full description of plates. The latter are clear and include the famous bronze plaques in the Ethnographical Collection at the British Museum. The letterpress refrains from aesthetic comment.

IV. *Aesthetics of African Indigenous Art*

19. RATTRAY, R. S. RELIGION AND ART IN ASHANTI. (Oxford University Press, 1927.) 30*s*.

An admirable and indispensable book, but dealing with Ashanti alone. The chapters on weaving are of first-rate practical importance and abundantly illustrated. The chapter on pottery is valuable but less complete. There is also a chapter on *cire-perdue* metal-casting with illustrations. The aesthetic side of Ashanti art is treated in a chapter by Vernon Blake, which is the most penetrating and profound study of the aesthetics of primitive art that we have found in any language. Vernon Blake, who died in 1930, was a sculptor and painter and a writer of distinction. He lived and worked among the indigenous peoples in Malaya,

China, and India, and therefore wrote with comparative knowledge. His essay is difficult and condensed, but no better analysis of the mind of the primitive artist has yet been written. He takes a somewhat pessimistic view of the immediate future of indigenous art under European and American influences. Tentatively he forecasts a change in the trend of modern European thought. His suggestion that there is a deep affinity between a submerged part of European thought and the thinking of primitive peoples is significant though speculative.

20. FRY, ROGER. VISION AND DESIGN. (Chatto & Windus, 1920.) pp. 65–8. 25s. Article on NEGRO SCPULTURE.

This short chapter [along with Vernon Blake's chapter entitled 'The Aesthetic of Ashanti' in Rattray's *Religion and Art in Ashanti* (see above)] is the best introduction in English to the whole subject.

21. RATTRAY, R. S. AKAN ASHANTI FOLK-TALES. (Oxford University Press, 1930.) 21s.

This book is illustrated by Africans of the Gold Coast Colony.

22. ROTHENSTEIN, WILLIAM. THE DEVELOPMENT OF INDIGENOUS ART. (*Oversea Education*, Vol. I, No. 1, October 1929.)

23. STEVENS, G. A. THE AESTHETIC EDUCATION OF THE NEGRO. (*Oversea Education*, Vol. I, No. 3, April 1930.)

Mr. Stevens's paper is of unique interest as recording the experience of a European teacher eliciting indigenous art expression from a class of West African pupils.

For Product Safety Concerns and Information please contact our EU
representative GPSR@taylorandfrancis.com
Taylor & Francis Verlag GmbH, Kaufingerstraße 24, 80331 München, Germany

www.ingramcontent.com/pod-product-compliance
Lightning Source LLC
Chambersburg PA
CBHW070731270326
41926CB00073B/3168

* 9 7 8 1 1 3 8 5 9 7 7 2 3 *